United States
Department of
Agriculture

Forest
Service

North Central
Research Station

General Technical
Report NC-254

Proceedings of the Great Lakes Silviculture Summit

I0411575

Acknowledgments

Great Lakes Silviculture Summit Development Team:
Louise Levy, Sustainable Forests Education Cooperative, University of Minnesota
Brian Palik, USDA Forest Service, North Central Research Station
Tom Crow, USDA Forest Service, North Central Research Station
Dan Gilmore, Department of Forest Resources, University of Minnesota
Janet Green, Minnesota Forest Resources Council
John Johnson, MeadWestvaco Corporation
Glen Mroz, School of Forestry and Environmental Sciences, Michigan Technological University
Linda Nagel, School of Forestry and Environmental Sciences, Michigan Technological University
Mike Walters, Department of Forestry, Michigan State University
Gary Wyckoff, MeadWestvaco Corporation
Eric Zenner, Department of Forest Resources, University of Minnesota

Great Lakes Silviculture Summit Invited Speakers:
Meredith Cornett, The Nature Conservancy of Minnesota
Linda Donoghue, USDA Forest Service, North Central Research Station
Kathryn Fernholz, Institute for Agriculture and Trade Policy, Community Forestry Resource Center
Jenna Fletcher, Minnesota Forest Resources Council
Bernie Hubbard, Michigan Department of Natural Resources
John Johnson, MeadWestvaco Corporation
Alan A. Lucier, NCASI, Inc.
Glenn Mroz, School of Forestry and Environmental Sciences, Michigan Technological University
Jack Rajala, Rajala Companies
David D. Reed, School of Forest Resources and Environmental Sciences, Michigan Technological University
James Sanders, USDA Forest Service, Superior National Forest
Robert S. Seymour, Department of Forest Ecosystem Science, University of Maine
Darrell Zastrow, Wisconsin Department of Natural Resources

List of Research Responders:
Dan Gilmore, University of Minnesota
Arthur Groot, Canadian Forest Service
Craig Lorimer, University of Wisconsin-Madison
Dave Morris, Center for Northern Forest Ecosystem Research
Linda Nagel, Michigan Technological University
Brian Palik, USDA Forest Service, North Central Research Station
Bill Parker, Ontario Forest Research Institute
Reino Pulkki, Lakehead University
Mike Walters, Michigan State University
Eric Zenner, University of Minnesota

Proceedings of the Great Lakes Silviculture Summit

Compiled and Edited by

Brian Palik
USDA Forest Service, North Central Research Station
Grand Rapids, MN 55744
bpalik@fs.fed.us

Louise Levy
Sustainable Forests Education Cooperative
University of Minnesota
Cloquet, MN 55720
llevy@umn.edu

Contents

The Great Lakes Silviculture Summit: An Introduction and Organizing Framework

About The Authors:

Brian Palik, Project Leader, USDA Forest Service, North Central Research Station, Grand Rapids, MN; e-mail: bpalik@fs.fed.us.

Louise Levy, Project Leader, Sustainable Forests Education Cooperative, University of Minnesota, Cloquet, MN; e-mail: llevy@umn.edu.

Thomas Crow, National Program Leader, USDA Forest Service, Research and Development, Washington, DC; e-mail: tcrow@fs.fed.us.

Introduction

In recent years, institutional commitment to silviculture as a research discipline has decreased in the Great Lakes region and elsewhere. Ironically, at the same time, the various demands placed on silviculture by users of research have increased greatly and continue to do so today. There remains the need to produce more and better quality wood and fiber, a need heightened by an increasing population. In addition, silviculture is called upon to restore degraded ecosystems, to increase ecological complexity and diversity in production systems, to restore and manage ecological reserves, and to ensure that forests are managed sustainably for a wide array of ecosystem goods and services including aesthetic quality, recreational opportunities, and non-timber forest products.

There is a long history of production-oriented silviculture research in the Great Lakes region and beyond, and some methods of increasing volume yield of wood fiber are well documented. However, there is still much to learn. In particular, the synergistic effects of doing everything just right to maximize productivity in an intensive silvicultural system (e.g., fertilization, irrigation, spacing, superior genotypes, competition control, thinning) have not been well quantified for Great Lakes timber species.

Silvicultural strategies that target sustainability of a variety of ecosystem benefits and values are greatly underexplored. These approaches might be designed to optimize wood production along with other ecosystem attributes, such as native species diversity or riparian functionality. Or, the goal may be to maximize production and sustainability of ecosystem attributes other than wood fiber. More focus is also needed on production of quality sawtimber and veneer from the variety of species that are native to the Great Lakes region.

Finally, we have come to better understand the role of natural disturbances in regulating forest ecosystems, but we also know that allowing nature to take its course is rarely possible in our human-dominated landscapes. This is true even in the context of managing ecological reserves and natural areas. In fact, such areas may have great need for silvicultural intervention, perhaps for restoring or sustaining ecosystems in the face of altered natural disturbance regimes (e.g., suppression of natural fire). While research on silvicultural strategies for ecological reserves is ongoing, often taking the form of restoration ecology or prescribed fire research, the role of silviculture in reserve management warrants further attention.

A Model For Framing Silvicultural Research Needs

One conceptual framework for organizing silvicultural research needs is a model that arrays stand management objectives along a gradient of management intensity and desired

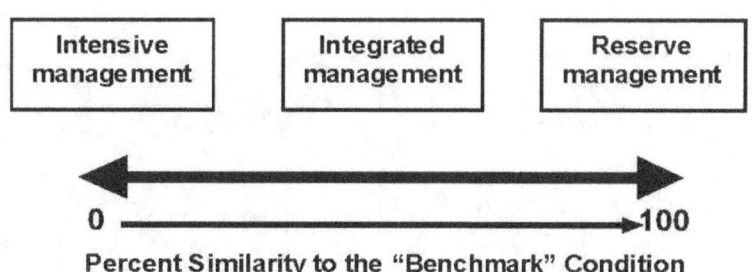

Figure 1.—Conceptual model for evaluating silvicultural needs relative to management goals and desired future conditions.

1

future conditions (fig. 1). On the right end of the gradient is the unmanaged, benchmark condition. This may be the condition of choice if management of ecological reserves is the primary objective; hence we refer to this as the domain of reserve management. Research needs at this end of the gradient may include approaches for restorating historical composition and structure or eradicating and controlling exotic species. The left end of the gradient is the intensively managed condition. An extreme example is a short-rotation, single-cohort plantation of an exotic species, where maximization of fiber production is the sole objective. We refer to this extreme as the domain of intensive management. Silvicultural research needs for intensive production might include optimizing spacing, thinning, and competition control to maximize growth while minimizing costs. There is a wide array of conditions between the ends, falling within the domain of the model we call integrated management. These conditions could include, for example, extended rotation, single-cohort, single-species stands or multi-cohort, mixed-species stands. The point is that managing for extractive timber objectives is one of many goals and one that becomes less important, relative to other ecological goals, as we move to the right along the gradient, toward the domain of reserve management. Research

needs in this domain include testing approaches for adding ecological complexity (e.g., of structure or composition) to stands managed for wood production, or projecting the effects of this added complexity on production levels (Palik and Zasada 2002).

When applied to whole landscapes, the nodes of our model (intensive, integrated, and reserve management) suggest a land allocation approach similar to the "triad" model of Seymour and Hunter (1999; and see Seymour, this volume). Under the triad model, a landscape contains both production forests and ecological reserves, embedded within a forest matrix that is managed to conserve biological diversity. Some stakeholders have interpreted the matrix condition to be homogeneous with respect to management approaches and conditions, with management for diversity and complexity given priority. In application, the matrix forest will be managed in many different ways. Some approaches will focus on conservation of biological diversity and ecological complexity, with wood production being a secondary and minor objective. Other approaches will favor fiber production, but with some consideration for sustaining biological diversity (i.e., more so than with true intensive production). The examples are limitless, as suggested by the gradient in figure 1. When translated into a landscape perspective, the resultant model suggests a spectrum (fig. 2), where

Figure 2.—A spectrum model of forest land use allocation in which production and reserve forest are embedded within a matrix managed for integration of ecological and production goals. How these goals are balanced varies greatly across the matrix.

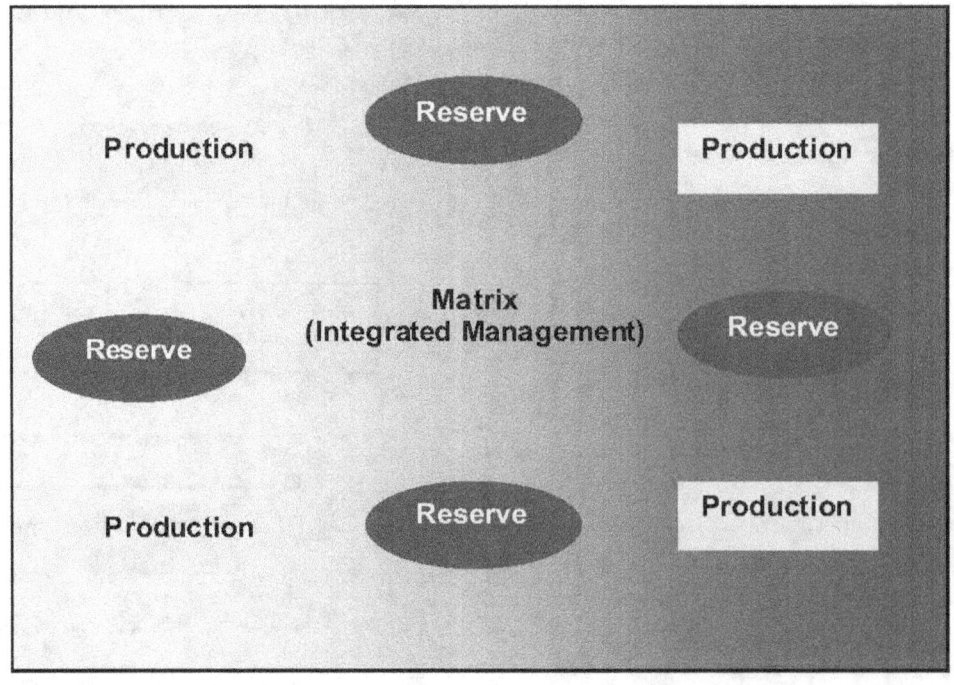

approaches and goals grade into one another. Some portions of the matrix are managed in similar ways to production forests (closer to yellow on the spectrum), and some portions are managed to favor goals and conditions similar to reserve forests (closer to blue on the spectrum), again, with a wide array of options for balancing ecological and production objectives between the ends.

The Challenge and Goals of the Great Lakes Silviculture Summit

To address the challenges and opportunities suggested by the spectrum model (fig. 2), silviculture research must become more multidisciplinary and broader in its scope and perspective. To do so, researchers need a better awareness of the range and complexity of the silvicultural needs of the stakeholders in the region. The Great Lakes Silviculture Summit, which took place in April 2003 at Michigan Technological University, was conceived with this need in mind. The primary audience of the summit included organization representatives who define needs and set policy on silvicultural approaches and practice, as well as researchers working in silviculture or related disciplines, i.e., those who can help meet the needs.

An overarching goal of the summit was to develop and strengthen a collaborative research network within the Great Lakes region that focuses on silvicultural information needs of various user groups, i.e., those that implement silviculture on the ground. A first step in developing this network was to obtain a clear message from organizational decisionmakers about their information needs. User group presenters at the summit were selected specifically to represent organizational needs from across the management spectrum (fig. 2). Representatives of regional research institutions were asked to respond to user group presentations by summarizing their current or planned research capacity to address stated needs. The specific objectives of the Great Lakes Silvicultural Summit were to:

1. Bring together silviculture and related researchers and decisionmakers from organizations that use this research;
2. Present the pressing issues facing the users of silviculture in the Great Lakes region and beyond;
3. Outline the capability and capacity of researchers to address these issues;
4. Chart a research agenda for the future that addresses user needs.

Our desired outcomes for the summit included clarification and articulation of the present and future status of silvicultural needs and capabilities in the Great Lakes region. We were also interested in developing stronger collaborative relationships among researchers whose work focuses on or is directly relevant to silviculture. Finally, our goal included the development of a research agenda from topics identified and endorsed by summit participants.

Some of these goals and desired outcomes are addressed in the following series of papers. In the first paper, Bob Seymour provides an articulate synthesis of the development of silviculture as a discipline. This synthesis examines where silviculture research is now, where it needs to go in the future, and by extension, what is silviculture in the 21st century? The next paper, by Dave Reed, examines the context of silviculture in the Great Lakes region. What is the current state and what are the recent historical trends in area, growing-stock volume, and utilization of Great Lakes forests? In examining these trends, we should be in a better position to consider issues and opportunities that need to be addressed by silviculture in the first decades of the 21st century. The following four papers are drawn from the user group presentations. These papers synthesize the silvicultural needs of i) *the pulp, paper, and dimensional lumber industries* (Alan Lucier); ii) *conservation organizations* (Meredith Cornett); iii) *non-industrial private landowners* (Kathryn Fernholz); and iv) *quality saw log and veneer industry* (Jack Rajala). (Note: additional presentations were made by representatives of State and Federal forest management. Although these papers are not included, their comments are incorporated into the research agenda found in this volume.) The next paper, by Tom Crow, synthesizes what we learned from the summit presenters about information needs, capabilities, and the future direction of silviculture research in the region. Finally, we distill what we learned from presenters and participants, including comments from a panel of institutional representatives (see appendix) and respondents during small-group breakout sessions, into a research agenda for silviculture in the Great Lakes region.

Literature Cited

Palik, B.; Zasada, J. 2003.
An ecological context for regenerating multi-cohort, mixed species red pine forests. Res. Note NC-382. St. Paul, MN: U.S. Department of Agriculture, Forest Service, North Central Research Station. 8 p.

Seymour, R.S.; Hunter, M.L., Jr. 1999.
Principles of ecological forestry. In: Hunter, M.L., Jr., ed. Managing biodiversity in forest ecosystems. Cambridge, UK: Cambridge University Press: 22-61.

Silviculture: Lessons From Our Past, Thoughts About The Future

Introduction

Silviculture has always been a keystone of American forestry, but to many, it seems, this discipline has lost its relevance during the past decade or so. In some regions, silviculture has become unfairly equated with production forestry, leaving a perceived void that forest ecologists or other specialists have attempted to fill, I would argue, somewhat unsuccessfully. In reality, most silviculturists see production forestry as but one of many applications of silviculture, and in the past decade, many have embraced paradigms involving conservation biology, natural disturbance patterns and processes, and management for structure rather than yield. Yet silvicultural research, on both traditional and contemporary issues, has waned as the USDA Forest Service and other organizations have refocused on other more topical issues.

This paper traces the evolution of silvicultural doctrine and practice over the 20th century, with emphasis on paradigm shifts that at their times were embraced with enthusiasm, but that now, in retrospect, often seem to be excessive oscillations of the pendulum. These paradigm shifts define the endpoints of four distinct periods in North American silviculture, each of which is characterized below. In this historical reflection, I will draw heavily from the wide-ranging interview of David M. Smith conducted by Harold Steen (1990) published during the year of Professor Smith's retirement. Professor Smith has been an eye-witness to more than half the 20th century, learned from and knew well those who defined the first half, and arguably has had more influence over American silviculture than any other individual. It was a great honor and privilege to be one of his students. Contemporary attempts by silvicultural scientists to maintain the vitality of our discipline are discussed. I conclude with some observations about how silvicultural research, a necessarily long-term endeavor, can respond to the needs of today's and tomorrow's foresters and society.

The Custodial Era (ca. 1900-25)

During this period, American foresters had essentially two concerns: keeping wildfires from causing further devastation, and ensuring regeneration after logging, the latter usually beyond their control. Tending operations and other hallmarks of intensive silviculture were almost nonexistent.

One early silviculture text was authored by Carl Schenck (1912), instructor of the short-lived forestry program on the Biltmore estate of George Vanderbilt (now the Pisgah National Forest) near Asheville, North Carolina. Schenck recognized that natural regeneration was critical and the only feasible way to ensure forest renewal; he attempted to adapt what he termed "fixed European methods (of regeneration)" to the more "primeval" forest of America. He observed that regeneration methods, or "types" as he called them, can be classified using six different criteria: relative position of the old and new growth; size of the regeneration units; degree of exposure of new seedlings; timing of seedling establishment relative to the timing of logging; presence of competing woody vegetation; and number and distribution of "standards" (reserve trees from the previous cohort).

Schenck went on to categorize all regeneration methods into one of three types based on whether natural regeneration develops after, simultaneously with, or before, timber harvesting. Today, we could describe these as clearcutting or seed-tree, shelterwood, or overstory removal (release of advance growth), respectively. Within each of these methods, he

About The Author:

Robert S. Seymour, Curtis Hutchins Professor of Forest Resources, Department of Forest Ecosystem Science, University of Maine, Orono, ME; e-mail: Seymour@appollo.umenfa.maine.edu.

distinguished four basic variants based on the size of the regeneration units: entire compartment (stand), strips, groups, or "selection" (small patches). Each of the 12 permutations was then described in some detail, but it is obvious that he preferred shelterwood and systems based on advance growth for American conditions and eschewed clearcutting for most applications. I find this structure eminently logical, because it does not associate stand age structures with the ecological process of seedling establishment; for example, there is no "selection" method of regeneration.

For better or worse, Schenck's approach to silviculture never caught on. The growing preeminence of the Yale Forestry School, with its close connection to Gifford Pinchot and the USDA Forest Service, ensured that whatever was taught there would become influential. The first edition of "The Practice of Silviculture" (Hawley 1921)—a text that survives today into the nineth edition (Smith *et al.* 1997)—is usually regarded as the seminal work on American silviculture. In this work, Hawley insisted on simplifying regeneration methods into only a few basic types, and it is here that the long-standing convention of naming entire (rotation-long) silvicultural systems after the regeneration method (i.e., the shelterwood *system*) became established (Hawley 1921, p. 11). According to Dave Smith, this was a conscious decision by Hawley, done to emphasize the major stewardship issue of the era, timely regeneration after logging.

Actually, the idea of simplification, and the distillation of systems themselves from their more elaborate European progenitors, was not original with Hawley; this basic classification first appeared in Graves' (1911) classic "Principles of Handling Woodlands." In the preface, Graves noted, somewhat apologetically, "I have laid special emphasis on some of the more primitive methods of forestry because these are often the only methods which can be applied under conditions of poor markets and difficult

logging. Thus, a prominent place is given to the selection system in its first application to virgin forests; …"

The custodial period also witnessed the first systematic documentation of the ecology and silviculture of North American trees and associated communities. The USDA Forest Service assigned research foresters to each important region, and by the 1910s, they began to publish comprehensive monographs on tree species and important silvicultural issues. In my own region, the spruce-fir forest of northern New England, the research forester was Marinus Westveld. Even today, one cannot work in a region very long without recognizing the lasting legacy of these pioneers. For example, Westveld's (1931) synthesis on spruce-fir regeneration is as valuable today as 70 years ago. These early works included little, if any, formal research as we now know it, yet they are full of timeless information. These early foresters were skilled naturalists as well as professionals fully engaged in the issues of the time. Their writings not only provide an important window into the past, they remind us that honed powers of observation are as important as carefully designed studies.

The "Selective Cutting" Era (ca. 1925-60)

As the forestry profession grew, the National Forest System became well established, old-growth forests grew scarce in the East, and "experiment stations" were established in every region to address topical silvicultural issues. By this time, the profession had almost universally embraced selection cutting as a universal panacea. In part, this was a strong reaction against clearcutting, because this form of logging had become so closely associated with exploitation that any support of its legitimate applications would have threatened the profession's growing public support and mandate. Indeed, Bernhard Fernow at Cornell learned this lesson the hard way when he tried to create spruce plantations in the Adirondacks; the New York Legislature eliminated his forestry program, and Yale, not Cornell, is now recognized as the Nation's oldest forestry school. There is little doubt that these early researchers were heavily influenced by the influential work of F.E. Clements (1916) on plant succession. The structure and function of the "climax forest" became a ruling doctrine, and silviculture that deviated from natural succession by interjecting disturbance was rarely considered.

Selection cutting also had a strong appeal beyond its putative ecological underpinnings. Practically, it seemed to be the only way to conserve some growing stock in the rapidly dwindling area of virgin forest where most of America's wood still stood. Logging systems for partial cutting and markets for anything but large, high-value trees were poorly developed or nonexistent. Thus, researchers eager to provide positive alternatives to clearcutting naturally began to install large trials of various partial cutting approaches on the growing body of experimental forests throughout the country. These trials were largely empirical studies of growth and yield as well as demonstrations of alternative logging methods. The fundamental dynamics of managed selection stands—most notably, the timely recruitment of desirable regeneration that would ensure stand sustainability—were rarely considered, and as we will see below, this oversight ultimately proved to be their undoing.

The attempts at selection cutting were not limited to the last remnants of eastern old growth; they were also enthusiastically embraced in the Pacific Northwest Douglas-fir region where forests remained largely unexploited. Unlike eastern North America, the Pacific Northwest was still dominated by high-volume old-growth timber, and if there was ever any place where stand sustainability was irrelevant and gap-phase regeneration inoperative, it was here. Yet this did not stop what we now see as a badly misplaced attempt at selection management that went on for decades (Munger 1950).

An important positive legacy of this era was the nationwide establishment of experimental forests that were devoted to large trials of various silvicultural systems (Ostrom and Heiberg 1954). Many of these survive and even thrive today, especially where the original trials included even-

aged systems that were distinctly unpopular at the time. For example, Dave Smith once told me that the original plan for the Penobscot Experimental Forest did not include the shelterwood method. In response to Smith's comments, two shelterwood variants were added, and today, these are among the most useful and widely applied systems by landowners (Seymour 1995).

Near the end of this era, authorship of "The Practice of Silviculture" passed to David M. Smith. Smith was strongly influenced by his mentor and graduate advisor, Harold Lutz, who in turn had studied under Yale's pioneering forest ecologist, James Toumey. On the occasion of his retirement in 1990, Smith confided that he was driven by Lutz's concern that in order for silviculture to survive, it must become more scientific and less empirical. As junior author of the sixth edition (Hawley and Smith 1954), Smith began the process of revising Hawley's largely didactic approach to silviculture into one founded on its growing ecological underpinnings, a change that was not complete until the seventh edition (Smith 1962). Smith (pers. comm.) also indicated that he never lost sight of Hawley's admonition, viz. that if silviculture is ever to be relevant in America, it must become profitable. This is perhaps why Smith's texts have become so valuable: successful silviculture is all about balancing the ecological and economic, and one cannot read Smith's persuasive writing without embracing this philosophy. As this era drew to a close, the pioneers ended their careers, but not without publishing important monographs (e.g., Eyre and Zillgitt 1953, Westveld 1953) that have become classics and remain influential.

By the 1950s, the negative legacy of the selective cutting era was becoming increasingly apparent (Seymour et al. 1986). Poor markets and limited logging technology had too often led to high grading via diameter-limit cutting; smaller d.b.h. classes had not been tended, and regeneration had often been ignored. If one now doubts this history, one needs to look no further than the recommendations for white pine management in the Lake States contained in R.H. Westveld's (1949, p. 315) regional silviculture text:

> "Selection cutting is recommended for mature white pine stands, because it perpetuates the type most effectively and economically. Approximately 75 to 80 percent of the volume of the stand should be removed (Zon 1928). Included in the trees that are cut should be the largest trees of all species, except a few white pines over 15 inches dbh wherever seed-bearing trees are deficient, and most of the hardwoods unless they are well adapted to the site...."

Such inattention to forest renewal and sustainability did not sit well with the stewardship ethic of the forestry profession. Entire landscapes dominated by mismanaged stands fueled an urgency to do something different.

The Multiple-Use, Production Forestry Era (ca. 1960-1990s)

I cannot trace from the literature exactly when and where the sea change occurred, but beginning ca. 1960, the Forest Service abandoned the doctrine of selection cutting and mandated that even-aged silviculture take its place, in virtually every forest type, everywhere, on the U.S. national forests (Boyce and Oliver 1999). Regime change, we would now call it, hit the forestry profession square in the forehead.

It was unmistakably during this era that silviculture became equated with production forestry. The post-World War II prosperity and housing boom, combined with continuing forecasts of timber scarcity, underscored the importance of the U.S. national forests as the Nation's wood basket. I cannot forget being repeatedly inculcated with the dogma *"What's good for timber is good for multiple use"* when I was a forestry student in the early 1970s. Much of forestry—extending through teaching, research, and practice—became dominated by an agricultural paradigm following successes in agronomy. This was a hopeful, upbeat era; rather than recognizing

this paradigm for the millstone it would become, we embraced it with unbridled euphoria. Major scientific advances in genetics, weed control, stand tending, sampling, and growth prediction suggested that American silviculture had finally emerged from the dark ages. Growing trees in plantations or simplifying natural stands to homogeneous even-aged structures was seen as the highest form of practice; shelterwoods, however sophisticated, were regarded as lame holding actions until management intensified; and selection cuttings survived mainly as experimental trials on research forests.

In the Eastern U.S., silviculturists were called upon to produce silvicultural guides for many forest types. Included in each guide was an elaborate decision tree, in which the only outcomes were either (1) a balanced uneven-aged stand managed by a B-d-q structure or (2) a single-cohort stand regenerated by complete removal cuttings (e.g., Marquis 1994). Other feasible structures, especially two-aged ones that have strong natural precedents in many forests and that just plain make sense in many management situations, were not legitimized. Although there is much useful information in these guides about silvics, stocking, and regeneration, I believe this "cookbook" approach to silvicultural prescription effectively codified a stifling form of silviculture, and for this reason, I have never used them in my teaching. Interestingly, these guides are now being reassessed and revised, at least in some regions, to better reflect a wider range of possible stand structures and management objectives ranging from production forestry to restoration and conservation of ecological reserves (Gilmore and Palik, in press).

As much as he disliked the abuses of the selective cutting era (see p. 143-191 in Hawley and Smith 1954) and welcomed the new openness to even-aged silviculture, Dave Smith (1972) also foresaw and warned us about the danger ahead for naively believing any single silvicultural system is appropriate for all conditions. At that point, citizens had already begun to resist very public manifestations of the agricultural paradigm that took the form of terracing on the Bitterroot National Forest in the late 1960s. And there was much more resistance to come: the Monongahela controversy and the spotted owl, to name a couple of prominent examples.

Some time during the 1980s, leading silviculturists began to realize that just growing trees well, by whatever means necessary, was no longer enough. In the mid-1980s, Chad Oliver organized a series of papers published in the *Journal of Forestry* that challenged us to reflect on the past and look to the future. Critical introspection on these articles, my own included (Seymour *et al.* 1986), reveals that we were neither sufficiently prophetic nor honest with our colleagues and ourselves about the need for reinventing silviculture. Oliver (1989) was also responding proactively to another threat to silviculture: the increasing specialization of forestry faculties, and the devaluing of silviculture as an important, integrating, and academic discipline. He decried the trend of replacing retiring silviculturists with specialists focused only on scientific performance—"hyphenated silviculturists" as he called them—who were saddled with teaching the undergraduate silviculture course but did research in soils, ecology, or biometrics.

By the late 1980s, the profession's ignorance or disregard for noncommodity values of forest ecosystems on public forests increasingly had placed it at odds with society, whose increasing affluence began to value natural forests as much as cheap plywood and dimension lumber. By putting all of our silvicultural eggs in one basket, in many regions we were caught with egg on our faces: bereft of proven silvicultural systems that accommodate aesthetics, public uses, and natural ecosystems, and lapsing into tired rhetoric about "educating the public" in a futile attempt to change its value systems. Challenges to production silviculture were dismissed by its proponents as a nostalgic plea to return to the abuses of the selective cutting era, as if only two choices existed, rather than an opportunity to invent a new way.

Ever resilient, however, the progressives among us rallied to keep us relevant. In retrospect, a milestone was Jerry Franklin's (1989) plea for a "new forestry," which inspired the Type B foresters (sensu Aldo Leopold) who had heretofore been in the closet, while inciting the entrenched Type A's to dig in (Atkinson 1992). Chris Maser's (1990) book "The Redesigned Forest" unquestionably was influential in challenging the status quo in the Pacific Northwest, and in turn, the country. This debate, still very much ongoing, has caused the maturing forestry profession to reexamine its core values. It should come as no surprise that silviculture— where forestry meets the land—is at the heart of this introspection.

The Balanced Forestry Era (1990 - ?)

I write this section with some trepidation, because there is certain arrogance in trying to capture history as it unfolds, especially when one has attempted to influence its course while the outcome is still unclear. I was originally tempted to call this section "a return to our ecological roots," but this is not all that is happening. Rather, I like to believe we have learned and grown from the turmoil of the past decade and have come to view silviculture as a broadly inclusive, inherently diverse discipline that society will once again come to value for the ecological and commodity benefits it can produce (O'Hara *et al.* 1994).

The concept of a "balanced" forestry was first outlined in Seymour and Hunter (1999) as a chapter in a compendium about managing forests for biodiversity. Put simply, balanced forestry explicitly acknowledges that there is no single "right" way to manage all forests and make everybody happy. Further, and more controversially, it asserts that some forests should not be managed at all, but rather be retained humbly in their natural state as inspirational and scientific benchmarks against which to gauge our human interventions on the remaining landscape. Finally, with respect to the silvicultural schisms of the late 1980s, it attempts to validate both production forestry and ecological forestry and offers a way in which they may coexist in a win-win environment. Balanced forestry would be manifested on the landscape as a triad of ecological reserves and production forests, embedded in a matrix managed to conserve biodiversity.

The decade of the 1990s witnessed an explosion of influential literature, but now that the dust has begun to settle on this transition, two contributions stand out. The first was Mac Hunter's (1990) publication of "Wildlife, Forests, and Forestry," in which he introduces the concepts of biological diversity and conservation biology to foresters in a familiar, empowering fashion. One cannot read Mac's seminal book without having the reaction, "This stuff isn't so hard; I can do this. Thanks for giving me all the reasons I should." If others with less understanding and acceptance of foresters and forestry had written such a book first, then foresters might have come to view these subjects more as threats to be vanquished rather than as critical additions to our scientific roots.

The other major contribution I credit to Chad Oliver, who more than any other individual, brought disturbance ecology into the forefront of silvicultural thinking with his seminal 1981 paper. By documenting voluminously a myriad of examples of how the world's forests respond to and develop after disturbances, he reinforced the natural ecological basis of silviculture, which clearly had been fading into empiricism. His subsequent book, "Forest Stand Dynamics" (Oliver and Larson 1990, revised in 1996), further defined and described four major stages of natural stand development (initiation, stem exclusion, understory reinitiation, old growth) each with familiar silvicultural analogues. The emphasis on cohort initiation, as it responds to various types, intensities, and frequencies of disturbance, strongly reinforces the fact that silviculture based on natural disturbances is both ecologically grounded and inherently flexible. Because many possible silvicultural pathways exist for nearly all forests, all of which have natural precedents, locking onto any single pathway (e.g., single-cohort) needlessly hamstrings the practice of silviculture.

Other noteworthy additions to the contemporary silvicultural literature during the past decade include Ralph Nyland's (1996) silviculture text, which continually reminds us that silviculture has strong ethical underpinnings if we choose to find them. Barrett's (1995) "Regional Silviculture" also was revised for a third edition, making a strong attempt to discuss non-commodity issues in each region. "The Practice of Silviculture" entered its ninth edition, now coauthored by three of Dave Smith's most successful offspring. Kohm and Franklin's (1997) book captures well the sea change in the Pacific Northwest, and Chapter 7 (Franklin et al. 1997) details the important development of variable-retention harvesting. Most recently Lindenmayer and Franklin (2002) published the first book about landscape ecology that is accessible to foresters. This book relegates silviculture largely to a single chapter entitled "Matrix Management in the Harvested Stand," virtually all of which is about how to mitigate clearcuts. Issues with multi-aged forests, the most common natural structures in the humid temperate zone, including many of the Lakes States' forests, receive only five short paragraphs of attention.

Clearly, the forests of the Lake States and North-eastern U.S. demand not more ways of mitigating clearcuts, but diverse alternatives to them. As an example of how ecologically based silvicultural systems might be devised for our multi-aged forests driven by gap dynamics, I offer a recent publication of my own (Seymour et al. 2002) that allows silviculturists to judge the "naturalness" of any silvicultural system relative to gap size and disturbance return interval. This paper would not have been possible without the pioneering work of Craig Lorimer, silviculturist at the University of Wisconsin, who over a very productive career has systematically and creatively studied the region's natural forests in ways that are extremely valuable for silvicultural application in the new ecological era.

Thoughts on Silvicultural Research

It is not lost on contemporary silviculturists that our discipline is not exactly popular today, as evidenced by the lack of financial and political support from its potential sponsors. A quick perusal of the recently released review of the Nation's capacity for forestry research (National Academy Press 2002) reveals the dominant role of the Forest Service, which provides 82 percent of all public sector funding. A quick scan of Forest Service Web sites for each research station reveals few "silviculture" projects, though many involve silvicultural treatments but eschew the word. Candid reflection suggests that our efforts of the last 15 years at controlling damage and reestablishing our identity have, at best, been a holding action.

I believe silviculturists must make greater efforts to become engaged in multi-disciplinary studies of important forest management issues. With this in mind, let me offer a few thoughts about how future silvicultural research might be directed toward this end. Some of these ideas are not original; they stem in part from the 1999 Yale Forest Forum on Silvicultural Research (Friedman and Guldin 2001, Wishnie et al. 2000) where the themes of sustainability, flexibility, and rigor were stressed.

- Studies should create wide, but experimentally controlled, gradients in (1) annual disturbance rates (i.e., cohort initiation); (2) spatial patterns (gaps vs. dispersed regeneration); and (3) permanent retention of biological legacies.
- We should not just cut, stand back, and measure; rather, we can hypothesize distinct silvicultural pathways (sensu Oliver and O'Hara in review) and test them in an adaptive management setting.
- We should include two kinds of reference benchmarks as controls: (1) comparable untreated stands (as usual), and (2) intensively managed monocultures of common species. The former allows us to see how well we can emulate nature; the latter tells us how much we sacrifice for noncommodity values. The latter also gives us an opportunity to continue to refine production silvicultural practices in ways that may correct their perceived ecological shortcomings.
- We must not monitor only growth and regeneration; studies of tree senescence, death, and afterwards, are also critical. Here, the work of Seydack (1995) and Seydack et al. (1995) is well worth studying.
- Wherever possible, paleoecological studies to characterize vegetation and disturbance

rates over the past several millennia should be included. Such studies are valuable not only as presettlement benchmarks, but more importantly, as signs of how vegetation responded to past changes in climate.

- Thinking ahead to application by practicing foresters, such studies should develop and apply area-based (not size- or d.b.h.-based) targets for stand structure. The resulting silvicultural systems should be based on planned cohort structures and their spatial pattern; it is past time to shed Graves' and Hawley's early insistence on emphasizing regeneration methods over other factors.
- We must not be constrained by the conventional economic wisdom of the time. Such studies should generate fundamental understanding of vegetation dynamics and not apologize for including treatments that may be "uneconomic." On the other hand, growing trees on long rotations may produce specialty products of such high value (e.g., spruce for instrument sound boards; tall white pines for ship masts and spars) that silvicultural systems thought not to be profitable could prove otherwise.
- Research should anticipate changes in forest age structure, species composition, and ownership, using visual, predictive models that capture the complex spatial and vertical structure within stands and across landscapes (e.g., McCarter et al. 1998). Such capability will help us look forward and guard against focusing on silvicultural issues that have only historical relevance. Dave Smith frequently emphasized that "once we understand the forest of the present, it is gone, and we're faced with a new, more perplexing one."
- Finally, silvicultural researchers should not lose sight of the fact that application of any silvicultural system requires a thoughtful and rigorous prescription process. Compare, for example, how

Magnetic Resonant Imaging systems have revolutionized the diagnosis of human ailments, against our present-day foresters who still go to the woods with their 10 BAF prism, a Biltmore stick, and maybe a 30-year-old stocking chart. Imagine if a forester could go to the field with a device like a "smart" digital camera that required only quick horizontal and canopy images to measure stand composition, density, and structure. One could take hundreds of such "plots" in the routine course of a stand exam, allowing the forester to concentrate on thoughtful observation instead of making measurements. Such a device could incorporate remote sensing data and use GPS to give data a spatial context. The resulting information could be linked seamlessly with expert systems that incorporate information about biodiversity as well as traditional growth and yield models.

The need for improving the efficiency of the prescription process is especially compelling in regions dominated by complex natural forests, where overly simple prescriptions driven by cookbooks with even-aged underpinnings do not conserve biodiversity as they could. We researchers must work with practitioners to develop simple and efficient ways to make prescriptions that do not simplify the forest itself. If we ignore this, or fail at it, northern forests will either be managed poorly—for example, by expedient diameter-limit cuts—or not be managed at all because "it's too expensive" to do right. The sought-after triad would thus degenerate to a biad like New Zealand, where the only active silviculture occurs in exotic plantations.

Conclusions

We must remember that silviculture is fundamentally an active discipline, and that, in the words of Chad Oliver (Wishnie *et al.* 2000), "No matter how issues develop in the coming years, we need to keep in mind that the role of silviculture is to inform and improve forest management." We learn most by tweaking the system, not merely by observing it. We have known things for centuries that ecologists are just discovering. James Toumey recognized this in 1928 when he wrote in the preface of his seminal silvics book,

> *"When biologists took their investigations of the relation of plants to the environment from the laboratory to the field, they found the silviculturist already there with the accumulated facts of a century of field work."*

But ultimately, it is not enough just to do good silvicultural science, publish it, and see that it gets applied. We must remember that it is not enough that the Ponderosa pines on the Bitterroot terraces have grown into thrifty 30-year-old stands. Silviculture will regain its deserved prominence only if we engage in solving problems important to society. We will struggle with this, but we must succeed, for the alternative of being characterized as a self-serving, arrogant bunch, allied only with commodity interests, serves the interests of no one.

Literature Cited

Atkinson, W.A. 1992.
Silvicultural correctness: the politicalization of forest science. Western Wildlands. 17: 8-12.

Barrett, J.W. 1995.
Regional Silviculture of the United States. 3d ed. New York, NY: Wiley and Sons. 643 p.

Boyce, S.G.; Oliver, C.D. 1999.
The history of research in forest ecology and silviculture. In: Steen, H.K., ed. Forest and wildlife science in America: a history. Durham, NC: Forest History Society: 414-453.

Clements, F.E. 1916.
Plant succession: an analysis of the development of vegetation. Publ. 242. Washington, DC: Carnegie Institute. 512 p.

Eyre, F.H.; Zillgitt, W.H. 1953.
Partial cuttings in northern hardwoods of the Lake States. Tech. Bull. 1076. Washington, DC: U.S. Department of Agriculture, Forest Service. 43 p.

Franklin, J.F. 1989.
Toward a new forestry. American Forests (Nov.-Dec.): 37-44.

Franklin, J.F.; Berg, D.R.; Thornburgh, D.A.; Tappeiner, J.C. 1997.
Alternative silvicultural approaches to timber harvesting: variable retention harvest systems. In: Kohm, K.A.; Franklin, J.F., eds. Creating a forestry for the 21st century. Washington, DC: Island Press: 111-139.

Friedman, S.T.; Guldin, J.M. 2001.
The future of silviculture research – thoughts from the Yale Forestry Forum. In: Beyond 2001: a silvicultural odyssey to sustaining terrestrial and aquatic ecosystems; proceedings of the 2001 National Silviculture Workshop; 2001 June 13-17; Hood River, OR. Gen. Tech. Rep. PNW-GTR-546. Portland, OR: U.S. Department of Agriculture, Forest Service, Pacific Northwest Research Station: 110-114.

Gilmore, D.; Palik, B. [In press].
A revised manager's guide for red pine in the North Central region. Gen. Tech. Rep. NC- . St. Paul, MN: U.S. Department of Agriculture, Forest Service, North Central Research Station.

Graves, H.S. 1911.
The principles of handling woodlands. New York, NY: Wiley and Sons. 325 p.

Hawley, R.C. 1921.
The practice of silviculture (with particular reference to its application in the United States). New York, NY: Wiley and Sons. 352 p.

Hawley, R.C.; Smith, D.M. 1954.
The practice of silviculture. 6th ed. New York, NY: Wiley and Sons. 352 p.

Hunter, M.L., Jr. 1990.
Wildlife, forests, and forestry. Englewad Cliffs, NJ: Prentice Hall. 370 p.

Kohm, K.A.; Franklin, J.F. 1997.
Creating a forestry for the 21st century. Washington, DC: Island Press. 475 p.

Lindenmayer, D.B.; Franklin, J.F. 2002.
Conserving forest biodiversity: a comprehensive multiscaled approach. Washington, DC: Island Press. 351 p.

McCarter, J.M.; Wilson, J.S.; Baker, P.J.; Moffett, J.L.; Oliver, C.D. 1998.
Landscape management through integration of existing tools and emerging technologies. Journal of Forestry. 96: 17-23.

Marquis, D.A., ed. 1994.
Quantitative silviculture for hardwood forests of the Alleghenies. Gen. Tech. Rep. NE-183. Radnor, PA: U.S. Department of Agriculture, Forest Service, Northeastern Research Station. 376 p.

Maser, C. 1990.
The redesigned forest. Toronto, CA: Stoddart Publishers. 224 p.

Munger, T.T. 1950.
A look at selective cutting in Douglas-fir. Journal of Forestry. 48: 97-99.

National Academy Press. 2002.
National capacity in forestry research. http://www.nap.edu/openbook/0309084563/html/R1.html

Nyland, R.D. 1996.
Silviculture: concepts and applications. New York, NY: McGraw-Hill. 633 p.

O'Hara, K.J.; Seymour, R.S.; Tesch, S.D.; Guldin, J.M. 1994.
Silviculture and our changing profession. Leadership for shifting paradigms. Journal of Forestry. 92: 8-13.

Oliver, C.D. 1981.
Forest development in North America following major disturbances. Forest Ecology and Management. 3: 153-168.

Oliver, C.D. 1989.
The 2030 forest: directions of silvicultural research. In: Proceedings of the fifth biennial southern silvicultural research conference; 1988 May 12-14; Memphis, TN. Gen. Tech. Rep. SO-74. New Oeleans, LA: U.S. Department of Agriculture, Forest Service, Southern Forest Experiment Station:15-22.

Oliver, C.D.; Larson, B.C. 1996.
Forest stand dynamics. New York, NY: Wiley and Sons. 520 p.

Oliver, C.D.; O'Hara, K.L. [In press].
Effects of restoration at the stand level. In: Stanturf, J.A.; Marsden, P., eds. Restoration of boreal and temperate forests. London, UK: CRC Press.

Ostrom, C.E.; Heiberg, S.O. 1954.
Large-scale tests in silviculture research. Journal of Forestry. 52: 563-567.

Schenck, C.A. 1912.
The art of the second growth or american sylviculture. 3rd ed. Albany, NY: Brandow Printing Co. 206 p.

Seydack, A.H.W. 1995.
An unconventional approach to timber yield regulation for multi-aged, multispecies forests. I. Fundamental considerations. Forest Ecology and Management. 77: 139-153.

Seydack, A.H.W.; Vermeulen, W.J.; Heyns, H.E.; *et al.* 1995.
An unconventional approach to timber yield regulation for multi-aged, multispecies forests. II. Application to a South African forest. Forest Ecology and Management. 77: 155-168.

Seymour, R.S.; White, A.S.; deMaynadier, P.G. 2002.
Natural disturbance regimes in northeastern North America – Evaluating silvicultural systems using natural scales and frequencies. Forest Ecology and Management. 155: 357-367.

Seymour, R.S.; Hunter, M.L., Jr. 1999.
Principles of ecological forestry. In: Hunter, M.L., Jr., ed. Managing biodiversity in forest ecosystems. Cambridge, UK: Cambridge University Press: 22-61.

Seymour, R.S.; Hannah, P.R.; Grace, J.R.; Marquis, D.A. 1986.
Silviculture: the next 30 years, the past 30 years. Part IV. The Northeast. Journal of Forestry. 84: 31-38.

Seymour, R.S. 1995.
The northeastern region. In: Barrett, J.W., ed. Regional silviculture of the United States. 3rd ed. New York, NY: Wiley and Sons: 31-79.

Smith, D.M. 1962.

The practice of silviculture. 7th ed. New York, NY: Wiley and Sons. 298 p.

Smith, D.M. 1972.

The continuing evolution of silvicultural practice. Journal of Forestry. 70: 89-92.

Smith, D.M.; Larson, B.C.; Kelty, M.J.; Ashton, P.M.S. 1997.

The practice of silviculture: applied forest ecology. 9th ed. New York, NY: Wiley and Sons. 537 p.

Steen, H.K. 1990.

David M. Smith and the history of silviculture. Durham, NC: Forest History Society. 126 p.

Toumey, J.W. 1928.

Foundations of silviculture upon an ecological basis. New York, NY: Wiley and Sons. 73 p.

Westveld, M. 1931.

Reproduction on the pulpwood lands in the Northeast. Tech. Bull. 223. Washington, DC: U.S. Department of Agriculture, Forest Service. 52 p.

Westveld, M. 1953.

Ecology and silviculture of the spruce-fir forests of eastern North America. Journal of Forestry. 51: 422-430.

Westveld, R.H. 1949.

Applied silviculture in the United States. 2d ed. New York, NY: Wiley and Sons. 590 p.

Wishnie, M.; Ashton, M.; Friedman, S.T.; Dunning, G. 2000.

The future of silviculture and applied ecology research – a summary of a forum exploring the evolving role of silviculture and silviculturists in the United States. New Haven, CT: Yale School of Forestry and Environmental Studies. Yale Forest Forum Series. 3(2): 40 p.

The Context For Great Lakes Silviculture In The 21st Century

Introduction

Great Lakes forests were subject to a severe pulse of disturbance from the mid-19th century through the early 20th century that resulted from extensive harvesting and subsequent fires following European settlement. Today's forest, in many ways, is exhibiting changes in area and demography that reflect recovery from this pulse of disturbance, as well as response to agricultural land abandonment in the region in the mid- to late-20th century. Management of these forests in the 21st century must take these trends into account, plus consider societal needs and expectations that are changing in response to population levels and other factors. Our knowledge base for managing these forests is limited, even with respect to such basic characteristics as productivity. We also have little historical reference on which to base new silvicultural systems designed to manage forests in response to emerging environmental issues such as global climate change.

The objectives of this paper are to review the current state and recent historical trends in area, growing-stock volume, and utilization of Great Lakes forests and to consider several issues and opportunities that will need to be addressed by silviculturists in the first few decades of the 21st century.

Regional Trends

Smith et al. (2001) present the most recently available, national information on the current state and historic trends in the forest resources of the United States. It is important to remember that the Great Lakes forest resource is responding to the same factors (earlier severe disturbance, increasing population, etc.) as forests in the remainder of North America, particularly in the Northeastern U.S. and southern Canada, although timing and extent vary by region. Great Lakes forests cannot be examined in isolation because many activities affecting future forests will be local manifestations of national and international trends.

The information presented here focuses on Michigan, Minnesota, and Wisconsin. This is not to shortchange other States, but these three States contain over 60 percent of the forest land in the North Central United States, and over a third of the forest land in the North Central and Northeastern U.S. (Smith et al. 2001). In these three States, forest area has been increasing in recent years (fig. 1), accompanied by a large increase in growing-stock volume (fig. 2).

About The Author:

David D. Reed, Dean of the Graduate School and Professor, School of Forest Resources and Environmental Sciences, Michigan Technological University, Houghton, MI; e-mail: ddreed@mtu.edu.

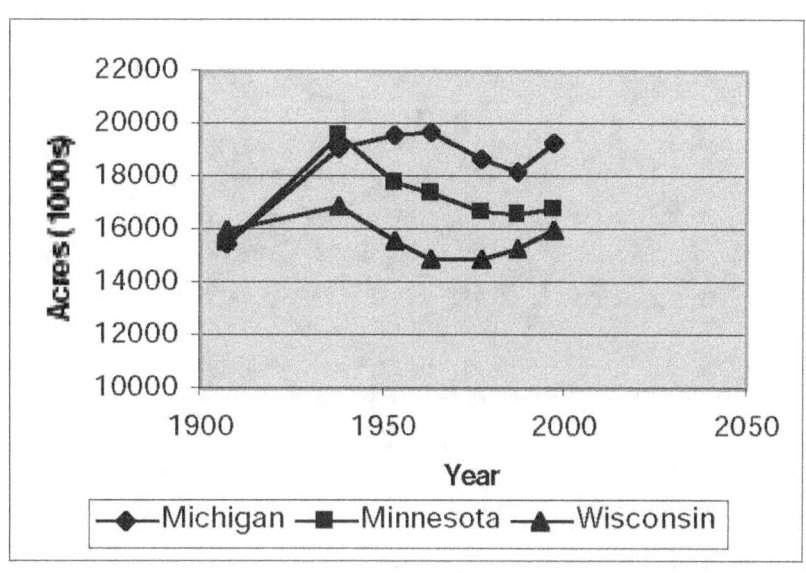

Figure 1.—Forest area (in millions of acres) in Michigan, Minnesota, and Wisconsin from 1907 through 1997 (source: Smith et al. 2001).

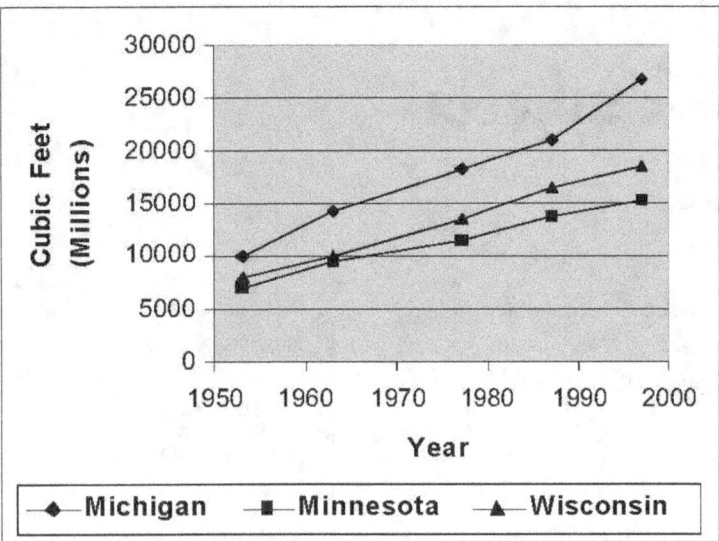

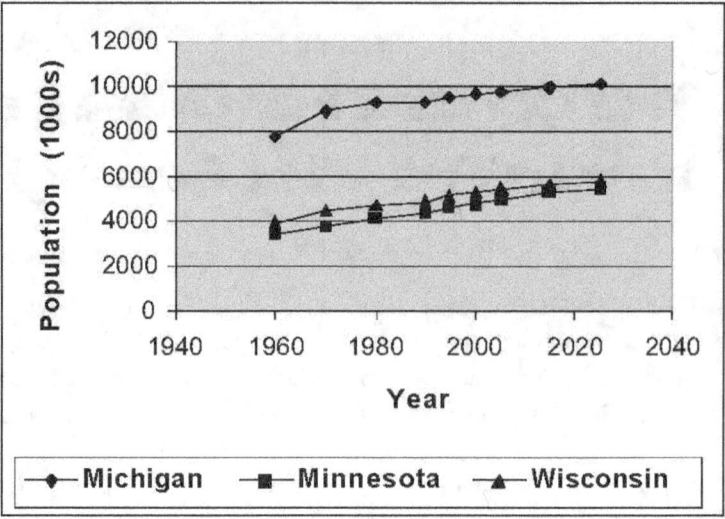

Figure 2.—Net volume of growing stock (in millions of cubic feet) in Michigan, Minnesota, and Wisconsin, from 1953-1997 (source: Smith *et al.* 2001).

Figure 3.—Population trends in Michigan, Minnesota, and Wisconsin since 1960 with projections through 2025 (source: U.S. Census Bureau).

Of the over 52 million acres of forest land in these three States, over 49 million acres (94%) is timberland[1], and 1.9 million acres (3.7%) is reserved, or withdrawn from timber utilization (Smith *et al.* 2001). Of the approximately 49 million acres of timberland, 5.9 million acres (12%) is federally owned, 13 million acres (26%) is in other public (State, county, and municipal) ownership, 3.4 million acres (7%) is owned by forest industry, and 27 million acres (55%) is owned by nonindustrial private landowners (Smith *et al.* 2001).

The national trends affecting the commercial utilization of wood produced on national forest lands have impacted these three States, but probably to a lesser extent than the rest of the country. The one area where the Great Lakes region is relatively unusual is in the amount of land in State, county, and municipal ownership. This largely can be traced to the means by which these three States

handled land that reverted to them through the failure of landowners to pay taxes during the depression in the 1930s. With the increasing population of the Great Lakes region (fig. 3), it remains to be seen whether there will be increasing controversy over commercial utilization from forestland in State, county, and municipal ownership.

From figure 2, it is reasonable to assume that an increase in net growing-stock volume will continue into at least the early decades of the 21st century. Population in this region is increasing and is expected to continue increasing in the coming decades; the impact of this increase in population on land use and societal expectations from Great Lakes forests is unknown, but could be great. It is clear that pressure on the Great Lakes forest resource is increasing, although it has not yet reached the levels experienced in other regions of the U.S. except possibly in Minnesota (table 1).

Forest Productivity

In such an environment, Great Lakes forest managers need to thoroughly understand forest productivity and ecosystem behavior to design and implement silvicultural systems to meet these challenges. Although the Great Lakes region was a pioneer in silvicultural research in the early and mid-20th century, it has lagged behind other regions in the last half of the last century.

---

[1] *Timberland is defined as forest land that is producing or is capable of producing crops of industrial wood and not withdrawn from timber utilization by statute or administrative regulation; areas qualifying as timberland are capable of producing in excess of 20 cubic feet per acre per year of industrial wood in natural stands. Currently inaccessible and inoperable areas are included Smith et al. (2001).*

Table 1.—Annual net growth, removals, and mortality in millions of cubic feet for Michigan, Minnesota, and Wisconsin compared to the Pacific Northwest, South, and South Central United States (source: Smith *et al.* 2001)

Growth component	State/Region					
	MI	MN	WI	PNW	South	South Central
Net growth	756	370	489	3,472	4,731	10,712
Removals + mortality	551	540	360	2,617	5,694	12,421
Difference	205	- 170	129	855	- 963	- 1,709

Around 1980, several large industrial corporations maintained research centers in the Southern and Western U.S. and university-industry research cooperatives were very active in other regions, including cooperatives focused on issues of forest productivity or growth, and yield. Cooperatives focused on such issues as spacing and thinning to maximize yield and studied the effects of such treatments on wood quality (e.g., the Loblolly Pine Growth and Yield Cooperative at Virginia Tech). At the same time, Forest Service research laboratories that focused on silviculture were being closed or consolidated in the Great Lakes region and university-industry research cooperatives were very small and struggled to maintain members and activity levels in the region. Many forest managers believed that everything necessary to manage Great Lakes forests was already known and available in publications such as Arbogast's (1957) marking guide or the management guides published in the 1970s by the USDA Forest Service, North Central Research Station.

As a consequence, investment in Great Lakes silvicultural research declined to the point today where, basic knowledge of such things as the potential productivity of Great Lakes species is not known because we have not conducted the fundamental research necessary to understand productivity of Great Lakes forest species. Results from elsewhere indicate that there is a great deal of unrealized potential in these forests, but we need to perform the basic experimental work to understand these dynamics.

In northern Europe, for example, studies such as the experiment at Flakaliden (http://www.spek.slu.se/forskning/flakaliden_en.htm#Näring, Bergh *et al.* 1999) in northern Sweden demonstrate that northern species have a great deal of unrealized productive potential. In that experiment, located at 64°N latitude, manipulation of water and nutrient availability led to an approximate tripling of yield in unthinned Norway spruce to a level roughly equivalent to 3.3 cords per acre per year. In southern Sweden, at 57°N latitude, similar treatments led to yields of 6-7 cords per acre per year. Similar experiments have simply not been conducted for Great Lakes species, and the yield potential of Great Lakes forests is unknown.

Carbon Cycling and Sequestration

Basic knowledge of the role of forests in the global carbon cycle is limited, and detailed knowledge about C cycling within given forest systems is only beginning to be developed. We do not know how to inventory ecosystem C content with known precision and certainly do not know how to conduct such inventories in cost-efficient ways. It is not clear what forests managed to sequester carbon should look like or how they should be structured. Table 2 presents some data from two European forests of similar species composition (Scots pine overstory, *Vaccinium*-type understory) and soil morphogenesis. In these two forests, one located north of the Arctic Circle and one in

Table 2.—Stand characteristics and carbon content for two European Scots pine forests separated by 16° latitude (source: Reed and Nagel, unpublished data)

Characteristic	69°N	53°N
Age	178	90
Trees (ha⁻¹)	442	292
Basal area (m² ha⁻¹)	11.2	24.5
Average height (m)	10	26
Average diameter (cm)	17	32
Overstory carbon (t ha⁻¹)	1.2	7.2
Total carbon (t ha⁻¹)	22.6	23.3

central Europe, structure of the overstory and sizes of individual trees vary dramatically while total ecosystem carbon content is virtually the same. A great deal of work is needed in developing methods to efficiently estimate ecosystem C content. Much additional work is needed to develop silvicultural systems that will allow us to still extract fiber while increasing C sequestration. Because most C in northern forests is belowground, the investigation of belowground processes, along with decomposition, is needed to develop management methods that can be used to meet society's need for reducing atmospheric carbon while still producing needed fiber. We should not forget that if such methods can be developed and if methods to rapidly assess total system C with known precision can be developed, there may be great potential for managers to obtain increased income through C storage credits. Today, though, such potential is limited by uncertainty and the inability to verify such storage levels.

Population Genetics of Managed Forests

North American forests have been actively managed for only a relatively short time, even though human impacts on forest structure and composition extend back to the beginning of the Holocene. Silviculturists have conjectured about the impacts of various treatments on forest population genetics. Dysgenic selection, for example, refers to the loss of "good" genotypes that could result after repeated

diameter-limit harvesting. To date, this understanding has largely been based on reasoned conjecture, not on actual genetic composition data. Now, with the advance of molecular genetic technologies, it is possible to collect and interpret data to directly test such concepts and to improve our understanding of the impact of various silvicultural treatments on forest population genetics. This requires interdisciplinary collaboration between molecular geneticists, population geneticists, and silviculturists, and is extraordinarily difficult. This capability, though, opens up an entire new frontier in our ability to understand forest structure and composition and will lead to greatly increased understanding in the coming years. New technology can lead to new conceptual advances, and the design of future silvicultural systems will inevitably begin considering such information as we progress through the 21st century.

Conclusion

To conclude, the above discussion has three major points:

- Great Lakes forest growing stock is increasing, but so is utilization and regional populations, leading to both increased opportunities for economic development and increased pressure on the land and resource base.

- The true productive capacity of Great Lakes forests is unknown, and a great deal of fundamental knowledge is needed to develop silvicultural systems to satisfy a wide range of rapidly evolving management goals.

- We do not understand forest ecosystems sufficiently well to design management systems to address emerging issues such as carbon sequestration, although emerging technologies offer a great deal of promise if interdisciplinary teams can be developed to investigate and translate scientific findings into management recommendations.

Literature Cited

Arbogast, C., Jr. 1957.
Marking guides for northern hardwoods under the selection system. Sta. Pap. 56. St. Paul, MN: U.S. Department of Agriculture, Forest Service, Lake States Forest Experiment Station. 20 p.

Bergh, J.; Linder, S.; Lundmark, T.; Elfving, B. 1999.
The effect of water and nutrient availability on the productivity of Norway spruce in northern and southern Sweden. Forest Ecology and Management. 119: 51-62.

Smith, W.B.; Vissage, J.S.; Darr, D.R.; Sheffield, R.M. 2001.
Forest resources of the United States, 1997. Gen. Tech. Rep. NC-219. St. Paul, MN: U.S. Department of Agriculture, Forest Service, North Central Research Station. 198 p.

Silviculture Research Priorities For Strategic Paper Fibers In The Lake States

About The Author:

Alan A. Lucier, Senior Vice President, National Council for Air and Stream Improvement (NCASI), P.O. Box 13318, Research Triangle Park, NC; e-mail: alucier@ncasi.org.

Introduction

The economic performance of the pulp and paper industry in North America has been weak for more than a decade. Factors affecting performance vary among industry sectors and regions, but generally include slow growth in demand, excess production capacity, and low prices.

To make matters worse, North American pulp and paper mills are facing tough competition from new production systems in the Southern Hemisphere. In general, these new systems have the latest manufacturing technology and associated benefits in operational efficiency and cost. Moreover, most of the new systems include highly productive plantations of desirable wood species such as eucalypts, acacias, and pines. These plantations provide significant competitive advantages to the mills they support. These advantages include low growing costs for land and labor; short haul distances for harvested wood; and excellent wood properties that reduce manufacturing costs and improve the quality of final products.

The Lake States pulp and paper industry has not escaped the adverse effects of global competitive pressures. Wood supply is one of several major concerns. Although wood is plentiful in northern sections of the Lakes States, there are serious concerns about current and future supplies of the "strategic fibers" that the region's papermakers need to produce world class products at competitive prices. Wood supplies from Federal lands declined sharply during the 1990s, resulting in substantial increases in prices for aspen and softwoods. Mixed northern hardwoods remain plentiful, but concern is growing about inadequate regeneration of preferred species (e.g., birch and hard maple) in natural stands.

Silviculture research has much to contribute to improving strategic fiber supplies and the competitiveness of the pulp and paper industry in the Lake States. This paper outlines silviculture research needs in the Lake States from the perspective of foresters associated with the pulp and paper industry. Research needs were identified through discussions with industrial woodlands managers and researchers with responsibilities in Minnesota, Wisconsin, and the Upper Peninsula of Michigan. It is clear that the region's strategic paper fibers include aspen, softwoods, northern hardwoods, and hybrid poplar. Research priorities vary among companies depending on the geographic location and fiber requirements of manufacturing facilities. As a result, the research priorities outlined below are a composite picture of the views of several companies and do not represent the views of any single company.

Aspen

Aspen is a high-value fiber for many pulp and paper mills in the Lake States. Compared to many other hardwoods, aspen has good fiber-to-fiber bonding characteristics, low lignin content, and high pulp yields. Aspen fibers help producers of printing and writing papers achieve desirable sheet properties such as high opacity, brightness, surface smoothness, and bulk.

Concerns about aspen supplies include high prices; the high incidence of rot and stain in wood from older stands; and uncertainty about long-term supply trends. Factors affecting supply trends include:

- increasing demand for aspen by producers of structural panels (oriented strand board) and other engineered wood products;

- public forest policies affecting the availability of existing aspen stands for harvest; and
- lack of silvicultural practice that fosters aspen regeneration and productivity.

Silviculture research has a critical role to play in efforts to sustain and enhance the aspen resource in the Lake States. Priority research topics for the pulp and paper industry include:

- Regeneration
  Near-term: Harvest prescriptions for increasing the aspen component in forest areas dominated by low-quality mixed hardwoods.
  Longer term: Genetic selection, breeding, biotechnology, and plantation establishment.
- Management of existing stands
  1. Growth and yield research, including studies of interactions among site quality, stocking, and fertilization.
  2. Wood quality research on the influences of site, age, stand density, and moisture stress on staining and decay rates.
  3. Research, development, and demonstration of options for improving wood quality and financial returns to growers by shortening rotations.
  4. Integration of silvicultural practices into cost-effective management systems.

Softwoods

The long fibers of softwood species are critical components of many paper and paperboard products. Long fibers greatly enhance the strength of a paper sheet (e.g., tear and burst resistance) and thus affect the performance of paper machines and final products in use.

Several mills in the Lake States use high-yield mechanical pulping processes to produce pulp for light-weight publication papers (e.g., for magazines and directories). White and black spruce and balsam fir are strategic resources for these mills because papermakers and their

customers value the smoothness, flexibility, brightness, and strength of mechanical pulps in which spruce and fir are the primary softwood components.

Pulp and paper producers have various opinions about the relative advantages of spruce and fir. Some feel spruce generally has better fiber properties and higher wood density/pulp yield. Others believe a mix of spruce and fir provides the best sheet properties. Lumber producers generally prefer spruce because fir typically has higher moisture content and thus requires more time and energy for drying. Papermakers and lumber producers both note that fir from older stands (e.g., > 60 years of age) typically has a high proportion of rot.

Fir is often more available than spruce in local wood markets in the Lake States. Spruce supplies in the Lake States declined dramatically in the early 1990s as a direct result of harvest reductions on Federal lands. Today, substantial quantities of spruce fiber are being imported into the Lake States, while substantial numbers of spruce stands in the region are declining in health and productivity due to overstocking and neglect. Spruce regeneration and growth on non-Federal lands are inadequate to improve the long-term supply outlook. Where spruce regeneration occurs, overstocking is often a problem.

Chemical pulp mills in the Lakes States use several softwood species including the spruces, pines, larches, and balsam fir. Species preferences, tolerances, and use patterns vary among mills depending on final products and local pulpwood market conditions. In general, the ability of chemical pulp mills to use several softwood species is attributable to two factors. First, chemical pulps are used in a wide range of bleached and unbleached products with various fiber requirements. Second, chemical pulping and bleaching remove lignin, color, and extractives from wood fibers, thus allowing production of pulps with high brightness from a variety of species.

Softwood supply is a critical strategic issue for most pulp and paper mills in the Lake States. Industry research priorities include:

- Strategic assessment of options for increasing softwood production and/or imports.
- Cost/benefit analysis of silvicultural options for maturing and over-stocked softwood stands on public and nonindustrial private lands.
- Development and testing of soft-wood silviculture options for forestry investors and land managers, including thinning and fertilization of pine plantations; further development and accelerated deployment of hybrid larch plantation systems; and economical options for increasing spruce and fir production in stands established by planting or natural regeneration.

Mixed Northern Hardwoods

The Lake States region has an abundance of mixed-species northern hardwood stands. Fibers from these stands are used in several bleached and unbleached paper grades after chemical pulping.

Pulpwood prices are typically much lower for mixed northern hardwoods than for other strategic fibers (e.g., the price for high-quality aspen is often 1.5 to 2 times greater than the price for mixed hardwoods). As a result, silvicultural prescriptions for northern hardwood stands are often influenced primarily by expected returns to sawtimber. It is important to note, however, that some producers of printing and writing papers strongly prefer birch and/or hard maple. Prices for birch/maple pulpwood have been increasing.

Although mixed northern hardwood is an abundant and relatively low-cost resource for pulp and paper mills, there are concerns about long-term supplies because natural regeneration success has been marginal to poor in many stands. Industry research priorities include:

- Deer management research leading to reliable predictions of time windows for successful hardwood regeneration at a landscape scale based on effective population control measures and knowledge of natural population cycles.
- Herbicide research leading to reliable and cost-effective treatments to control sedge grass and invasive species that compete with hardwood regeneration.
- Research leading to harvest prescriptions that promote regeneration of mixed stands of high-quality hardwoods and softwoods.
- Growth and yield research that enables value growth projection in hardwood stands as a function of site quality, stand density, and species composition.
- Better methods for analyzing uneven-aged stands in harvest scheduling models.

Hybrid Poplars

Research in the Lake States and other regions has demonstrated the great potential of hybrid poplar plantations as sources of raw material for pulp, biomass energy, and other uses. Hybrid poplar plantations are being established on an operational scale in parts of Minnesota, where excellent yields of high-quality fiber on good sites can provide sufficient economic returns to justify relatively high growing costs. Priority topics for silviculture research include:

- *Near-term*: Optimize weed control, stand establishment, tree nutrition, and integrated pest management systems (especially for defoliating insects).
- *Longer term*: Traditional selection/breeding and biotechnology research for genetic improvement of wood quality.

Concluding Remarks

Silviculture research is a core competency of the forestry profession. It produces new forest management technologies and systems that enable progress toward economic and ecological sustainability. The ongoing decline in silviculture research capacity in the United States is a serious threat to the Nation's forest ecosystems and forest products industry. Without silviculture research, forestry loses much of its long-term practical value and becomes difficult to distinguish from other disciplines.

The Lake States region has a long history of achievement in forest stewardship, but has fallen far behind other wood producing regions in recent decades. Scandinavia and other regions have proven that well-integrated systems of silvicultural practices applied on a large scale can produce enormous economic, ecological, and social benefits. These benefits include improvements in tree quality, forest health, product versatility, aesthetics, wildlife habitat, and jobs.

There is an urgent need to assimilate existing knowledge from around the world and produce new Web-based silvicultural guides for the Lake States. The guides should be highly visual and provide "complete recipes" for achieving a range of objectives from wildlife management to timber production. The guides should also describe the potential regional benefits of modern silviculture as a way of building support for long-term investments in forestry research, education, and policy development.

A renaissance in Lake States silviculture research coupled with forest policy initiatives at the State and regional levels could simultaneously improve regional supplies of strategic fibers and forest ecosystem conditions, both in the near term and in the long term. Sustainable improvements in strategic fiber supplies would enhance the competitiveness of the region's pulp and paper mills and the communities that depend on them.

Silvicultural Research Needs In The Lake States: The Nature Conservancy Perspective

Introduction

The largest conservation organization in the United States, The Nature Conservancy uses a number of collaborative, entrepreneurial tools to achieve its mission:

> To protect plants, animals, and natural communities that represent the diversity of life on Earth by protecting the lands and waters they need to survive.

Founded in 1951, The Nature Conservancy (TNC) focused its early efforts on land acquisition. Over the last 50 years, TNC has worked to protect over 98 million acres around the world. Today, TNC owns over 2 million acres, and we are 1 million members strong. As the organization has grown, so has the number of approaches available for biodiversity conservation. The use of silviculture to achieve conservation goals is an example of one science-based approach that is on the rise at TNC.

The Nature Conservancy and Forestry in the Americas

Over the last several years, TNC has become increasingly involved in active forest management on our own lands and the lands of our partners. Currently, it owns 250,000 acres of working forest land across the United States. Increasingly, timber production on TNC lands is certified through the Forest Stewardship Council (FSC). Internally, land managers earn their certification through the new Certified Resource Manager Program. Conservancy staff members serve on the boards of both FSC and the Sustainable Forestry Initiative.

To enhance our forest management capacity and that of our partners, TNC has developed a number of different forestry programs and tools. For example, the *Forest Management Network* (http://tnc-ecomanagement.org/Forest/) has provided a forum and ongoing support for the development and implementation of silvicultural practices that are compatible with biodiversity conservation. TNC staff and partners have taken advantage of this forum in over 30 landscapes in the United States and Central America. TNC's *Conservation Forestry Program* was recently launched with the goal of working in partnership with private landowners to promote the economic productivity of working forests while protecting the ecological health and natural diversity of the landscapes in which they occur. The program recently published a "Forest Operations Manual" that describes on-the-ground operations for making our forests healthier, more diverse, and more valuable places in the future than they are today. This manual is designed as a "how-to" book for conservation forestry (http://tnc-ecomanagement.org/Forest/Resources/#FstOpsManual). A number of other tools, such as a sample management plan and sample conservation easement, are available on the Forest Management Network Web site.

Some examples of the conservancy's early forays into the world of silviculture and timber management came from New England, including the Upper St. John River in Maine and the Atlas Timberlands Partnership in Vermont. Both projects are working forests with an emphasis on maintaining biological diversity. The Upper St. John River includes 180,000 acres of conservancy-owned lands purchased in 1999. Huber Resources is currently under contract as the land manager. The average annual harvest is 30,000 cords of saw logs and pulpwood. The Upper St. John is making

About The Author:

Meredith Cornett, Director of Conservation Science, The Nature Conservancy of Minnesota, Duluth, MN; e-mail: mcornett@TNC.ORG.

use of riparian buffer and core reserve areas to complement the working forest portion of this project. FSC certification is in progress. The Atlas Timberlands project is a partnership between The Nature Conservancy and the Vermont Land Trust. FSC-certified in 2002, this 26,000-acre project is the third largest private ownership in Vermont. Through carefully designed silvicultural strategies, the goal for these lands is to produce high quality sawtimber and long-term profitability in addition to maintaining biodiversity values.

TNC's silvicultural activities in the Upper Midwest have geared up more recently than those in Vermont and Maine. To date, projects in the Great Lakes area have taken place on a smaller scale than in other regions, but with the potential to grow over time. For example, The Nature Conservancy of Minnesota recently purchased 7,300 acres of lowland conifer forest at the headwaters of the St. Louis River. UPM-Kymmene is under contract to develop an ecological management plan for these lands. Louisiana Pacific (LP) holds the timber rights on approximately 450 of TNC's acres in the project area. TNC's forester, UPM-Kymmene's ecologist, and LP's contract foresters and loggers collaborated on a plan for the timber sale that met the needs of all parties. Early efforts have focused on retaining trees after harvest, sustaining ecological reserves, and protecting natural regeneration.

Silvicultural Research Needs in the Lake States

In the Lake States, and more broadly wherever the conservancy has forest interests, the use of silviculture to further our conservation mission is part of the organization's adaptive management framework. TNC is a science-based organization, and a number of silvicultural research themes have emerged as TNC ventures into the world of forest management including:

1. Silvicultural techniques based on natural disturbance processes
2. Maintenance of biodiversity while ensuring a sustainable rate of economic return
3. Forest management at the appropriate scale in partnership with multiple landowners
4. Consideration of landscape context and cumulative impacts of forest management

Silvicultural techniques based on natural disturbance processes

An example of TNC's efforts to base silvicultural practices on natural disturbance processes comes from the Chequamegon Bay watershed of northern Wisconsin, where the Wisconsin Chapter recently purchased 1,000 acres from Nekoosa Papers. Under the State's Managed Forest Law (http://www.dnr.state.wi.us/org/land/forestry/ftax/managed.htm), 860 acres of the Caroline Lake preserve will be managed as productive working forest land. The conservancy hired a local forester to develop a forest management plan for these lands, which are dominated by even-aged northern hardwood forest, a mixture of sugar maple, birch, and oak.

Northern hardwood ecosystems are driven largely by small gap-phase dynamics. The silvicultural systems for this preserve were designed to match the natural disturbance processes. Long-term management goals include the development of an uneven-aged structure typical of mid- to late-successional northern hardwood forests and the promotion of underrepresented species such as red oak, yellow birch, white pine, and hemlock. With an emphasis on crop tree release, the plan emphasizes variable gap sizes, ranging from 20 to 70 feet in diameter. To maintain a continuous canopy, prescriptions will avoid reducing basal area by more than a third during a single stand entry.

Research designed to develop silvicultural practices based on the timing, frequency, size, and pattern of natural disturbance processes for the spectrum of forest ecosystems in the Lake States is a priority for TNC. Our forested preserves and partnerships with other landowners represent potential research sites for testing hypotheses about management and natural disturbance processes.

Maintenance of biodiversity while ensuring a sustainable rate of economic return

The Manitou Forest landscape is a 100,000-acre region in northeastern Minnesota defined by the watersheds of the Manitou, Caribou, and East Branch of the Baptism River in the North Shore Highlands of Lake Superior. Like the Chequamegon Bay project, most of TNC's silvicultural work in the Manitou Landscape to date has focused on northern hardwoods. Major landowners in this landscape include Lake County, the Minnesota Department of Natural Resources, the USDA Forest Service, The Nature Conservancy, Potlatch, and the Wolfwood Corporation. Several of these landowners came together in 2000 to form the Manitou Collaborative, a partnership dedicated to working together on mutual land management goals.

Managing northern hardwoods in this landscape comes with a special challenge: this particular forest ecosystem is at the northern edge of the range for many component species. As a result, the stature of trees in this forest is diminutive, compared to northern hardwood systems in Wisconsin and Michigan. Moreover, sugar maple is susceptible to frost cracking. Through the help of a grant from Minnesota's Coastal Program[1], the Manitou Collaborative is partnering with researchers at the University of Minnesota to develop silvicultural systems tailored to the particular growing conditions of this landscape.

The goals of the Manitou partnership are twofold. Like its counterpart in the Chequamegon Bay project, the Manitou project strives to improve the ecological condition of northern hardwood ecosystems, such as increasing structural complexity and species diversity. The more challenging goal lies in designing silvicultural prescriptions that serve the dual purpose of managing for ecological attributes while producing quality sawtimber over the long term. The feasibility of achieving both ecological and economic goals for northern hardwoods in this landscape depends on the development of local markets for both intermediate and end products. Additional resources and expertise from TNC's Business Consulting Group will contribute to identifying solutions.

The lack of quality sawtimber and limited local markets for small diameter timber are not unique to the Manitou project. These and other challenges around the Lake States raise questions about how to develop silvicultural practices that both sustain or restore natural patterns of biodiversity and meet economic goals. As a community-based organization, TNC recognizes forestry as a centerpiece of the local economy. Unless silvicultural methods for working forests are economically viable, their usefulness for conservation is limited. We seek additional opportunities to partner on research on how to sustain the region's natural resource-based economy while maintaining biological diversity at multiple scales.

Forest management at the appropriate scale in partnership with multiple landowners

As with the Manitou Forest, a patchwork of ownership occurs at the Sand Lake-Seven Beavers landscape (named for two important lakes at the headwaters of the St. Louis River in northeastern Minnesota). The USDA Forest Service, Lake County, St. Louis County, the Minnesota Department of Natural Resources, and The Nature Conservancy have formed a working group to develop common management goals. The relationship among several of the partners was formalized through the signing of a Memorandum of Understanding in early 2003.

Before the working group was established, landowners each engaged in stand management without the benefit of understanding the larger landscape context. Past timber sales have been set up on the basis of ownership patterns, resulting in a cutting pattern that reflects ownership boundaries rather than natural patterns created by differences in soil, topography, hydrology, and past natural

---

[1] *This project was funded in part under the Coastal Zone Management Act by NOAA's Office of Ocean and Coastal Resource Management in conjunction with Minnesota's Lake Superior Coastal Program.*

disturbances. With the formation of the working group, there is potential for better coordination on land management in the future.

For example, rather than setting up several different sales for a 600-acre black spruce stand that spans four ownerships, a cooperative plan may be developed to manage the stand as a single ecological unit. Such an arrangement confers many benefits. Each partner saves on expenses. The operation would require fewer roads and would therefore be more efficient. Finally, this approach would foster natural patterns of regeneration designed to reflect what the land can best support, rather than the fragmentation that can result from uncoordinated management.

Managing at the appropriate scale and in coordination with other landowners also comes with a unique set of challenges, such as unaligned management planning cycles, interagency politics, and the logistics of managing land across ownership boundaries. Research in this new arena will help further the work of TNC and all land managers in developing approaches for sustaining multi-ownership landscapes.

Consideration of landscape context and cumulative impacts of forest management

For many project locations in the Lake States, TNC is using landscape context to inform stand management decisions, in an effort to better conserve biodiversity at multiple scales. Once landscape goals have been established, whether stand management decisions will actually meet those goals remains a vexing question.

To help find answers, TNC has begun research, through a project funded by the David H. Smith Postdoctoral Fellowship Program, to better understand ecological processes and cumulative effects of site actions in priority landscapes of the Great Lakes region. The project will develop modeling tools that help explore ways to enhance both biodiversity and timber values in large landscapes by adjusting the timing, type, spatial arrangement, and intensity of forest harvest and management activities. With the Manitou Forest landscape as a test case, the tools and principles

developed for this project will be broadly applicable to other landscape-scale forest conservation efforts.

Few tools and principles are available to help balance goals at both stand and landscape scales. Moreover, many are not user-friendly or are employed with little input from land managers. Research emphasizing the development of tools that help achieve land management goals at multiple scales is needed across the Lake States landscapes where TNC works with partners.

Conclusions

The use of silviculture as a conservation tool is on the increase for The Nature Conservancy. In recent years, the conservancy has invested heavily in working forest lands across the Nation, a trend expected to continue. TNC is eager to work with other researchers on testing innovative, ecologically based silvicultural practices in the landscapes where we work throughout the Great Lakes region. We also seek opportunities to partner with other landowners on mutually beneficial forest management projects within priority conservation areas.

Small-Scale, Private Lands Forestry In The Lake States

About The Author:

Kathryn Fernholz, Staff Member, Dovetail Partners, Inc., White Bear Lake, MN; e-mail: www.info@dovetailinc.org

Of the approximately 750 million acres of forests in the United States, approximately 46 percent is classified as "nonindustrial private forest" (NIPF). These are lands owned by private individuals, jointly or through family partnerships. According to the most recent USDA survey, there are 10,565,000 private woodland owners in the United States, collectively owning 392,731,000 acres of forest. The numbers also show that of these 10.5 million landowners, the vast majority own less than 50 acres. Specifically, 6.3 million own less than 10 acres and nearly 3 million more own between 10 and 50 acres (USDA 2003*).

*Note: these are preliminary data results; as the National Woodland Owner Survey pro-gresses, results with increasing geographic accuracy will be developed. The goal is to have reliable State estimates by the time the full survey cycle is completed in 5-10 years.

However, while the majority of landowners own few acres, a small population of large landowners own a large percentage of the total acreage. Specifically, about 2,000 individuals or families in this country own 28 percent of the Nation's private forest land (USDA 2003).

Approaches for Influencing Management on NIPF Ownerships

One challenge facing foresters and practitioners of silviculture is to find ways to facilitate forest management on private forest lands of varying sizes. A debate often arises over which lands and landowners to focus efforts on. There are at least two schools of thought on this. One emphasizes the scale of on the ground impact that is possible if efforts are focused on large landowners. The logic is that by reaching just 2,000 people, over one million acres can be affected. Management on this scale of ownership can accomplish many ecological goals, as well as help provide reliable sources of wood and fiber to support local and regional

Table 1.—Area and number of privately owned forests in the United States by size of forest landholdings

Size of forested landholdings (acres)	Area acres	Owners number
	Thousands	*Thousands*
1-9	20,033	6,343
10-49	63,295	2,965
50-99	43,287	641
100-499	99,216	556
500-999	24,290	38
1000-4999	31,678	20
5000+	110,933	2
TOTAL	392,731	10,565

Source: USDA Forest Service, Forest Inventory & Analysis, National Woodland Owner Survey, June 2003.

industries. Another school of thought is that efforts to assist private landowners should be focused on the small landholdings, such as those of less than 500 acres. The logic is that this represents the greatest numbers of individuals, citizens, voters, and community members. By reaching "the masses," the benefits are dispersed over a larger geographic area and more likely to create a domino effect. Additionally, due to their scale, these landowners often face more challenges in terms of commercially viable operations and access to traditional markets.

This debate over strategies to increase management on private lands is not a new one. There is no single easy solution or universally effective tactic when it comes to promoting forest management with private landowners, but we hope foresters are coming to realize there are many diverse and worthwhile approaches to consider.

Management Trends on NIPF Ownerships

Why it is important to promote forest management on private lands? Because NIPFs represent 46 percent of the total forestland in the country, they can exert significant influence on the forest product market and the availability of wood and fiber supplies. This same acreage represents 46 percent of the Nation's forest habitat and can exert a significant influence on wildlife, water quality, air quality, and other ecological and aesthetic considerations. Through appropriate forest management, NIPF lands are able to support local industries and jobs while also protecting environmental attributes that are strong determinants of community health. With this in mind, foresters don't have the option of ignoring NIPF lands. Clearly, as forest management practitioners, we need to be cognizant of how our science is made available and applied to private lands, as well as large industrial and public landholdings. However, current information shows that less than 5 percent of the country's NIPF owners, representing less than 15 percent of the NIPF acres, have a written management plan (USDA 2003). Although a much greater number of private landowners have "sought advice" from a variety of sources, without a written management plan it is difficult to

imagine that this management includes clear objectives, a silvicultural prescription, effective implementation, and appropriate follow-through. Without adequate professional assistance, private landowners are unlikely to receive maximum benefits, in terms of income potential, asset value over the long term, social and aesthetic values, and minimized negative environmental impacts.

Given the potential impact of forest management on private lands, we must ask ourselves why private landowners aren't more engaged in forest management. If we focus only on the northern region, defined as Maine to Maryland and west to Minnesota and Missouri, some interesting information comes out of the recent USDA survey.

This northern region includes about 5 million private landowners owning a total of nearly 130 million acres of forest land. For almost 2 million people, forest land is either part of their farm or their primary residence. The average landowner in the northern region has owned his or her land for about 25 years and is 60 years old (USDA 2003). From this information, we can already see that for many forest owners, the forest is their home, it has been their home for a large part of their adult life, and they most likely look at it out their kitchen window nearly every morning.

Further survey questions reveal that the primary reason for owning forest land is fairly evenly split between enjoying aesthetics, protecting nature, and having it as part of their residence. The lowest ranked reason, in the list of eight possible reasons, is nontimber forest products and just above that is timber production (USDA 2003).

These responses would appear to imply that landowners tend to be focused on the ecological and aesthetic benefits of forest ownership. However, of all the possible activities occurring on their ownerships, the most common is timber harvest (USDA 2003). About 10 percent of private landowners representing about 35 percent of the NIPF lands in the northern region have had a timber harvest in the past 5 years. Still, nearly one-third of the forest landowners in the northern region categorize their future plans as "no activity" or "minimal activity" (USDA 2003). These mixed signals tell us that while forest owners might not have timber harvesting on their list of things to do, when the markets are good or the opportunity or financial need arises, they are very likely to harvest their land, even if they don't always plan ahead for it.

Engaging the NIPF Ownership

With more than 10 million private forest owners in the Nation, it is unrealistic to think there is a one-size-fits-all answer to effectively reaching and meeting the needs of all those landowners. Instead, it is becoming increasingly important that landowners have a wide range of resources to choose from, including public agencies, private businesses, environmental organizations, community groups, and non-profits. It is more likely that landowners will find a source that they trust and are willing to work with to plan and implement their forest management. Although it is advantageous to have a wide range of resources available, the downside is the perception or reality of contradictory information being provided. Landowners may get conflicting advice or confusing information when they consult with more than one resource. Some landowners many simply pick one to believe over the others, while others may throw their hands up in confusion and give up. With the range of landowners needs and the range of resources available, it is increasingly important that natural resource professionals make every possible effort to fully explain their advice, provide landowners with adequate information to make an informed decision, and avoid undermining the efforts of other service providers. Although it is appropriate and fully expected that resource managers will disagree about forest management options, the basis for these disagreements should be explained to the landowners so that they understand that it is a matter of tradeoffs and not a clear cut case of only one right answer.

Various surveys over the years have illustrated the fact that trust is a major factor in determining what activities landowners are willing to engage in on their forest land. Landowners take their cues from what they see neighbors doing across the fence line and what they hear friends talk about at the café in town. For example, a recent survey of Minnesota's forest landowners found that getting advice from another landowner or neighbor was the second most common source of assistance, coming in just behind the Minnesota Department of Natural Resources (Baughman 2002). Resource managers should not underestimate or undermine the value and credibility of these methods of information exchange. There are four major areas of emerging opportunities, summarized below, for engaging the NIPF owners and improving management on their lands. All four of these rely at least in part on the development of trust and community-based information exchange.

Forest cooperatives

There is a renewed effort around forest landowner cooperation in the form of new generation cooperatives and landowner associations. These groups are not an attempt to replace or compete with existing and established forest landowner groups; instead, they represent a renewed interest in the values and motivating factors that were likely the origins of these other groups as well. In light of rapid community change and economic pressures and opportunities, forest landowners are seeing increasing opportunities and incentives for working with other community members to identify common interests, needs, and solutions. Cooperatives and landowner associations provide a variety of opportunities for increased forest management on private lands, a new avenue for delivering technical assistance and education to private landowners, and an additional point of contact between policymakers or researchers and forest landowners.

Forest certification

The evolution of forest certification systems represents a potentially revolutionary opportunity for forest landowners. If the development of certified organic agriculture is any indication, in 20 to 30 years we may have both a thriving certified forest industry as well as regional and local "forest farmers markets" where consumers are able to identify products that are grown and manufactured locally and are third-party certified through programs that challenge consumers to explore their values and make critical purchasing judgments. Certification provides some opportunities to improve private land management, but more importantly it provides an important tool for educating consumers, making them more aware of the impact of their purchasing decisions, and connecting them to their local forest resources.

Utilization standards

For a variety of reasons, the forest product industry has been changing its utilization standards fairly rapidly and significantly in recent years to accept a greater variety of species and grades. With changes in what the industry can utilize, what the market is demanding, and what customers are willing to pay, there are new opportunities for landowners to pursue more economically viable management alternatives and to help facilitate use of more diverse silvicultural methods. Specifically, with the development of more diverse hardwood markets, landowners in the Lake States are in a better position to apply management techniques such as crop tree management or uneven-aged management in some northern hardwood stands. Combined with increased nontimber forest product opportunities, these diverse markets will help more landowners recognize opportunities to participate in forest management activities that fit their values and ownership goals. However, like the other opportunities available to landowners, taking advantage of emerging markets is frequently a community effort relying on partnership and collaboration because of the economics of market access and operational feasibility.

Community identity

There is an increasing social and policy-level recognition of the value and community contribution made by healthy nonindustrial private forest lands. Community leaders, policymakers, and neighbors are increasingly recognizing that much of their local identity and sense of place relies on efforts made by private landowners to protect and enhance their forests. In some regions and countries, this recognition has resulted in innovative incentive programs that help reward and ensure that private landowners are able to maintain these resources. For example, Costa Rica has a program that provides direct payments to private landowners for environmental services such as air and water purification, carbon sequestration, and recreation (Snider 2003).

Silvicultural Needs on NIPF Ownerships

The critical silvicultural needs of the small private landowner relate less to identification of specific silvicultural tools and outcomes but more to the delivery of these tools and the availability of the expertise necessary to achieve desired goals. The management goals and, consequently, silvicultural needs of NIPF owners are inclusive of the full range of goals and needs outlined elsewhere in this volume, including management for quality wood products, management for fiber, and conservation and restoration of habitat and ecosystems. Knowing how to access information, implement prescriptions, and monitor the success of actions is the primary silvicultural need for NIPF owners.

Sometimes landowners are simply unaware of forest management options, sometimes they are unaware of the sources of assistance available to them, and sometimes they just don't know where to start. Additionally, the lack of available technical assistance is a growing concern; even when a landowner is ready to get started on management, the service providers are not readily available to provide assistance. We need more foresters on the ground providing services, and resource managers need to get more creative in finding ways to reach landowners. Field days, tours, Web sites, videos, and other methods will need to be used better in the future to both expand the impact of a limited number of resources and also try to reach the growing landowner population.

Resource managers also need to diversify the messages we give to landowners to enable us to reach a wider range of landowners and get them thinking about new ideas. To overcome the knowledge barrier, a renewed and continued effort is needed to develop educational materials and opportunities for private landowners. From brochures to booklets to workshops and training sessions, as much information as possible should be made available in as many formats as possible. To have the most impact, these educational resources should try to focus on actions, activities, and next steps that landowners can take to get involved or learn more.

To overcome the limited availability of technical assistance, efforts should be made to help landowners figure out what activities they can plan and execute themselves. Creating instructions for do-it-yourself projects or family projects related to forest management planning and providing training sessions on the necessary skills can help get more work done with fewer professionals. Examples might include chainsaw safety training, crop tree release, timber stand improvement marking and cutting, invasive species control, and direct seeding of hardwoods. These activities cover a range of skill levels, but most landowners are likely to have at least one area of interest and skill that they can apply with a little bit of direction.

Finally, a note needs to be made about silvicultural research. Too often, forest management research is conducted at a scale and intensity that is largely irrelevant to most private landowners. To engage landowners in the current science of forestry, efforts should be made to use citizen science for various monitoring projects, including gypsy moth, invasive and exotic plant species, and other forest health issues, as well as growth, yield, and stocking information. Efforts should also be made to actively utilize NIPF landowner partners in research. Using private lands and private landowners to contribute to the practice of forestry will emphasize the role these lands play in the landscape.

Throughout this discussion, the recurring theme is doing whatever it takes to engage a landowner and thereby making it possible to do more with less. An engaged landowner is much more likely to continue to tend the forest over the years and think of new projects over time. To create an engaged landowner, resource managers need to provide complete and accurate information and make sure their recommendations fit the scale of operations and needs of the landowner. In addition, guidance should be efficient in that it be fully developed and it must be effective in that it will result in recognizable changes or indicators of success. Finally, the costs and benefits should be accurately disclosed or estimated.

Private landowners exert a strong influence over the health of our forests, our forest-dependent wildlife, and our forest-dependent industries. The challenge we face now is working to ensure that the full range of management options and silviculture tools become available to the landowners of the region. The best way to keep forest management in the mix is to recognize the needs of private landowners and give them the tools to address those needs.

Literature Cited

Baughman, M.J. 2002.
Characteristics of Minnesota forest landowners and the Forest Stewardship Program. St. Paul, MN: University of Minnesota, Department of Natural Resources. 13 p.

Snider, A.G. *et al.* 2003.
Policy innovations for private forest management and conservation in Costa Rica. Journal of Forestry. 101: 18-23.

USDA Forest Service. 2003.
Forest Inventory & Analysis, National Woodland Owner Survey, 2002 Preliminary Results. (www.fs.fed.us/woodlandowners/results.htm).

Silviculture For Quality Forests: A Lumber And Veneer Perspective

Introduction

To the layperson (and sometimes even among professionals) there's a perception that forests are about big, old trees. A century ago certainly the forests of the Lake States con-sisted of large acreages of stands of mature trees that were both old and big. And even though there are remnant stands present today, settlement, development, and harvesting have caused numerous changes in the forest.

The lumber and veneer industry of the Great Lakes area was built to capitalize on these forests of large trees, and throughout the second half of the 19th century and well into the 20th, this was a major production area for the Nation's supply of both softwood and hardwood lumber and veneer.

A great deal has changed in the last 50 years. As the forest has changed, so has the industry. Today, there are far fewer lumber and veneer operations and most of the lumber production is from smaller trees. Just the same, there are still mills that focus on larger, higher quality sawtimber and veneer logs, and if not in quantity alone, certainly in quality, this production is a significant reason to manage for more high quality, large trees in our regional forests.

Additionally, the Lake States have seen a signi-ficant change in forest composition, which presents challenges as well. These biological challenges are significant in themselves, but the social/political issues that surround forest management today are equally as challenging. There must be both strong professional and community resolve around the belief that making the necessary commitments to and investments in forestry means that the forests then can be used to provide a full range of products and values.

The Changes

A great deal is known about the heyday of prime forests, logging, and big mills in the Great Lakes region. Heavy harvesting began in the 1830s and moved west across Michigan, Wisconsin, and Minnesota, cutting out 75 percent of the resource by 1930. It was an era that wasn't sustainable, nor was it ever intended to be. It wasn't until the late 1890s that concern about forest reserves brought about conservation efforts that have developed into our dedicated forests and public and private forestry organizations.

It is safe to say that over 1 billion board feet of sawtimber and veneer were harvested annually in each of the Lake States for many decades, and each State at one time held the record for the largest national volume harvested. Each State had a mill or two that broke national or international production records. For example, the Virginia Rainy Lake mill owned by Weyerhaeuser at Virginia, Minnesota, set a world record at 1 million board feet in 24 hours.

And, of course, the first and most sought after sawtimber was eastern white pine. Early writing indicated that the forests were thought to be eternal (endless), thus the name of the Minnesota book: "The Eternal Pines." Ultimately, Michigan and Wisconsin were more fortunate than Minnesota because when the pines were mostly gone there, underneath or along side these monarchs were rich hardwood forests.

Today, we have only a remnant left of that huge industry. Average yearly lumber production in the three States combined is less than 1 billion board feet, and more notably, production at standard sawmills (carriage and/or head saws), where quality lumber is produced, is only 25 percent of this total. Veneer production is also a fraction of former output.

About The Author:

Jack Rajala, President, Rajala Companies, Box 578, Deer River, MN.

So, where are we today in terms of capacity and supply; what has changed?

- Mills are fewer and smaller.
- Log supply is extremely tight and severely limits growth. Reasons are both biological and political.
- Wood quality (including size) continues to deteriorate.
- The shift to greater percentage of smaller diameter wood provides nothing for the veneer mills and very little for the quality lumber mills.

Some of the factors causing these changes include:

- Lack of timber management direction and output goals at major agencies
- Political influences
- Changes in cover types with a trend to pulpwood species
- Lack of sound silviculture consistently implemented on the ground

Throughout most of the last 30 years, the biggest constraint to growth of the sawtimber and veneer industry, and the major business challenge, has not been markets, nor manufacturing complexi-ties, nor even financial capital. It has been timber supply. And this is in a region where we have over 70 million acres of timberland. Has it been a lack of sheer volume of trees available? Only partially, and certainly forest land managers often struggle to have the budget and other resources available to keep lands productive and our forests healthy.

Then there's the huge challenge to keep forest land accessible. There are repeated and increasing attacks from detractors, alarmists, and anti-management groups who have tried all methods to stop the growing, the harvest, and use of trees for products. They have politicized the process of managing forests to an alarming extent.

But just as critical as these other challenges is the shaping of professional attitudes and cultures within the policymaking, scientific, and practitioner ranks. It's understandable that there will always be debate at the policy level about what, how much, where, when, and for whom. But this need not be paralyzing. And it's also understandable that science doesn't always give us a single, definitive answer, yet its validity must be honored. And it's understood that there is a broad menu of practices to choose from, once one has developed the policy, done the science, and is prepared to go out and practice forestry. At this point, all should be good to go. All systems clear. And yet, it often appears that the results have been far short of the mark, as reflected by the following:

- Stocking and productivity in many cover types are dismal in comparison to the quality and potential of sites.
- Forests are not healthy and trending downward.
- Tree and stand quality are far below par, resulting in fewer quality logs.
- Forests today increasingly cannot satisfy the resource needs of a modern sawmill/veneer and wood products economy.

A Need for More Change

So what, more precisely, is the answer? The answer largely revolves around our silviculture and how we use it and allocate it on the landscape.

A number of models are used to generalize the management of forests from a landscape perspective. One is the triad model (Hunter and Calhoun 1996) that differentiates manage-ment options in a triad of three categories, consisting of production management and reserve management embedded in a matrix of ecological or integrative management (fig. 1).

Figure 1.—Nodes of the triad model including production management (where fiber production is predominant), reserve management (where preservation of native biological diversity is the priority), and extensive or integrative management where commodity production and sustainability of biological diversity are shared priorities.

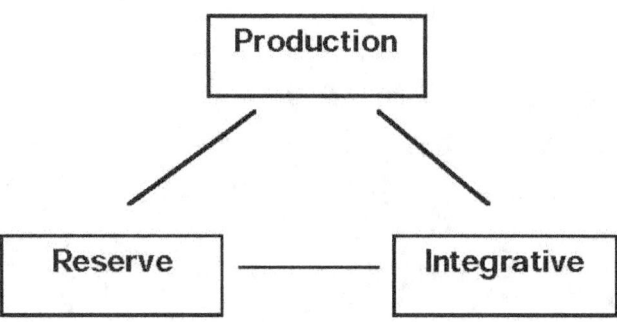

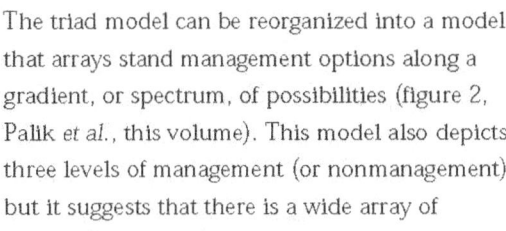

| Production management | Integrative management | Reserve management |

Figure 2.—A spectrum or gradient of stand management options ranging from production management to management of ecological reserves.

The triad model can be reorganized into a model that arrays stand management options along a gradient, or spectrum, of possibilities (figure 2, Palik et al., this volume). This model also depicts three levels of management (or nonmanagement), but it suggests that there is a wide array of options for integrative management.

Many times, forest landowners and professionals/ managers are caught between the two vocal and competing extreme ends of the spectrum. Meanwhile the middle ground has become narrower and smaller. We've heard the point again and again. If we very intensively manage part of the forest (likely short-rotation, single-cohort, single-species stands), that will take care of all the product needs and then much more of the forest can be preserved in an undisturbed state where natural forces will sustain biological diversity. And the vice-versa rationale is also often heard. The result of all this one-end-or-the-other posturing has greatly diminished the middle ground the very ground that should be most fertile for the silviculturist. This is the area of greatest management challenge and opportunity. Whereas it's relatively easy to do intensive, short-rotation forestry, and it takes no great management skill to just leave forests alone, managing forests that are diverse in composition and complex in structure calls on the best of the science and art of silviculture. Further, it is this integrative middle ground of forest management that provides the stands that give us the sawtimber and veneer logs that are in such short supply. The simple fact is that the sawtimber/ veneer industry cannot survive if it must go head to head with global producers of commodities from intensive managed forests, if it tries to live on small diameter trees, and if it is locked out from a wood supply because the forest is simply put into ecological reserves.

A New Emphasis

The hope for the producers of wood products (quality lumber and veneer) is to call upon silviculturists to use their fine science and art for growing and tending forests to produce quality trees and at the same time sustaining forests in terms of their compositional and structural diversity, wildlife habitat, scenic beauty, recreation, and just plain great nature.

It seems quite clear; just the same, in a recent technical report (Shifley and Sullivan 2002) on the state of the region's forests, we see an interesting quandary. The report says that in the North Central Region we have 17 percent of the Nation's population and 14 percent of its timberland. The region consumes 17 percent of the Nation's wood, grows only 10 percent, and harvests only 7 percent. The same report goes on to say "There are many ways to alter the current balance among growth, harvest, and consumption." Interestingly, the suggested menu of things that resource managers can do includes:

- Increase forest growth per acre through improved management of natural forests.
- Increase growth per acre through intensive plantation culture.
- Increase the number of forested acres in production through tree planting and agro-forestry.
- Change the amount of wood sold.

Note that all of these suggestions are quantitative prescriptions and miss the mark of promoting better trees for higher yield, quality, and value. Once again, we sense the lack of perception that it's not just a matter of more; it's also a matter of more what and to be sure, it's a matter of how. That's where good silviculture really counts.

A New Goal

The silviculture model needs to be reshaped to expand (not compress) the complex and sensitively managed forest section firmly in the middle, and it's time to provide the silvicultural concepts, strategies, practices, and tools to make our management far more holistic.

At either end of the spectrum model (figure 2, Palik et al., this volume), a whole lot of the wood industry will falter and disappear. It's in the middle area, the managed forest area that we will find the quality resource that is the solid foun-dation of the wood products industry. It's here in the center of the spectrum that we have the greatest silvicultural challenges and opportuni-ties.

Some examples of the more notable silviculture opportunities that could help expand and improve the management of our forests:

1. Develop a modern silvicultural program to return management of red pine on appropriate sites in long-rotation, multi-cohort, multi-species stands. This can be done by developing stands composed of released or residual red pine, grown to full maturity, while a new cohort com-posed of a variety of species develops underneath. An alternative red pine strategy could save managers from relying solely on an 80-year rotation, single-species, even-aged regime, which can be undesirable ecologically and economically.

2. Find viable ways to restore white pine to the landscape. Interest in white pine as both an economically and ecologically important species has grown, but white pine, for numerous reasons, has suffered serious population decline and now occupies only a fraction of its former presence. These reasons for the decline are fairly well understood, but a comprehensive silvicultural approach to successfully manage this species on a widespread basis has not yet been developed.

3. Demystify and simplify hardwood management systems so they are readily understood and easily implemented. Within the Lake States, managing hardwoods can be one of the most challenging tasks modern forestry confronts and the results for the most part show it. There is a steady decline in both acres and quality in hardwood cover types. From a product stand point, quality means both tree size and clear wood, or in biological terms, longer growth and/or faster growth. Further, it means healthy, well-formed trees. A large amount of silvicultural literature is available today that addresses the issue, but unfortunately, it is either not easily disseminated or user friendly. It is far too little used, especially in Minnesota. Many professional land managers, both private and public, do not have a plan for managing northern hardwoods; rarely do they have a plan for white birch or even for red oak.

4. Develop an alternative management system for aspen that allows it to be grown in multi-species, multi-cohort, longer rotation regimes. Aspen management is generally thought of as single-species, short-rotation management. It has worked well in the Lake States. In many areas the site and historical composition could favor other cover types, but because aspen is so competitive and easily, cheaply regenerated the site stays in aspen. The result has been a tremendous increase in the aspen cover type in the region at the expense of other types. The silvicultural challenge is to manage aspen as part of mixed-species, multi-cohort stands, in an attempt to grow trees bigger and make them more valuable for lumber and veneer.

In summary, silviculture can help grow big trees of high value and utility, and it needs to do it in an ecologically sound and sustainable way. Oh yes, and also in an economically efficient way.

Literature Cited

Palik, B.; Levy, L.; Crow, T.R. 2004.
The Great Lakes silviculture summit: an introduction. In: Palik, Brian; Levy, Louise, eds. Proceedings of the Great Lakes silviculture summit. Gen. Tech. Rep. NC-254. U.S. Department of Agriculture, Forest Service, North Central Research Station: 1-4.

Shifley, Stephen R.; Sullivan, Neal H. 2002.
The status of timber resources in the North Central United States. Gen. Tech. Rep. NC-228. St. Paul, MN: U.S. Department of Agriculture, Forest Service, North Central Research Station. 47 p.

Silviculture In The New Age Of Conservation

Introduction

In his seminal book "The Practice of Silviculture," Smith (1962) compared the role of silviculture in forestry to agronomy in agriculture. Both are applied sciences dealing with managing ecosystems for human benefit. Silviculture is, as Bob Seymour notes in this volume, "where forestry meets the land." What is the relevance of traditional silviculture in an era of managing for multiple values as opposed to multiple uses? Do we need a "new silviculture" as suggested by terms like New Forestry, New Perspectives, Adaptive Management, and Ecosystem Management? What are the important gaps in knowledge about silviculture in the Lake States? How might silviculture contribute to conserving biological diversity, promoting ecosystem health and sustainability, improving forest aesthetics, and enhancing nontimber forest products?

These and many other questions were explored at the Silviculture Summit hosted by Michigan Technological University in April 2003. In my synthesis of these discussions, I explore a premise—that the emphases in silviculture on regenerating trees and on optimizing growing stock at the stand level are not sufficient by themselves to ensure ecological diversity, forest health, and sustainability at the stand level, and importantly, at levels beyond the stand. If this premise is proven, a corollary follows: to meet the broad objectives of ecological diversity, forest health, and sustainability, it is necessary to move beyond the false dichotomy of even- vs. uneven-aged silviculture.

Premise: Traditional Silviculture Has Landscape-Scale Consequences

The premise has to do with issues of scale, spatial relationships, and forest dynamics. During the past several decades, a model of forest dynamics has emerged in which forested landscapes are viewed as patchworks of individual stands at various stages of development ranging from stand initiation to old growth (Oliver and Larson 1996). The stand initiation stage follows disturbance in which a new population or cohort of trees becomes established. The stem exclusion stage is next and it is characterized by intense competition that limits tree regeneration. A third stage, understory reinitiation, occurs when the original cohort begins to decline and reductions in canopy density allow understory vegetation to establish and develop. The increases in structural complexity that occur during this stage—e.g., multi-layered canopies, the occurrence of coarse woody debris in many sizes and stages of decay, canopy gaps of varied sizes—begin to resemble an old-growth forest.

Under a regime of natural disturbances, these dynamics produce a landscape in which all stages of stand development are present at any given time. It is this variation in conditions that creates habitat (ecological) diversity that sustains ecosystem health (Aplet et al. 1988). Silviculture applications affect these spatial and temporal patterns, but the cumulative impacts of many individual silvicultural applications conducted at the stand level are poorly understood at the landscape level. Take the case in which no forest in the landscape is allowed to develop beyond rotation age. Doing so will effectively truncate the process of stand development and thus preclude any forest in the landscape from obtaining old-growth status. In hemlock-dominated stands in Wisconsin and Michigan, as an example, characteristics relating to tree density, tree sizes, diameter-age relations, and occurrence of logs in advanced stages of decay were related to a

About The Author:

Thomas R. Crow, National Program Leader, USDA Forest Service; Wildlife, Fish, Water, and Air Research; Washington, DC; e-mail: tcrow@fs.fed.us minimum stand age of 275 to 300 years (Tyrrell and Crow 1994). For these forest ecosystems, stands that were 100 or even 200 years did not contain all the structural features that characterized a 300-year-old forest. When stand development is truncated, the result is a forested landscape that is less diverse than that expected under historical natural disturbance regimes.

Spatial relationships are receiving more attention in resource management because the composition, size, shape, and relative arrangement of spatial elements all affect the benefits and values that can be derived from the landscape. In one such application, Franklin and Forman (1986) evaluated the landscape-level implications of the staggered-setting system of clearcutting used on Federal lands in the Pacific Northwest. By interspersing small clearcuts within the matrix of continuous forests, the abundance of high contrast edges in the landscape increased dramatically, resulting in greater susceptibility to windthrow even after a relatively small proportion of the landscape had been harvested. A spatial pattern commonly resulting from human activities is fragmentation—that is, human activities tend to create small patches from large patches on the landscape (Bratton 1994, Mladenoff et al. 1993, Riitters et al. 2000, Wade et al. 2003). The point here is that land use creates landscape patterns that have social, economic, and ecologic significance, but our understanding of these relationships is rudimentary at best.

Corollary: The False Dichotomy Of Even- Versus Uneven-Aged Management

The work by Oliver and Larson (1996) on disturbance ecology and forest development provides the basis for the corollary—moving beyond the false dichotomy of even- vs. uneven-management (also Seymour, this volume). The full spectrum of stages of stand development, they argue, needs to be incorp-orated into a silvicultural system to produce a landscape in which all stages of forest devel-opment are present. The potential derivations in silvicultural applications available under the general rubric of Integrative Management, i.e., the conceptual region between Reserve Management at one

extreme and Intensive Management at the other extreme, in the model presented by Brian Palik et al., and reviewed by Jack Rajala (this volume), seem almost unlimited. Viewing silvicultural systems and their related regenera-tion methods as static and rigid defies the richness and variety represented in ecological systems, the numerous environmental services provided by forests, and the basic human needs derived from these services.

Managing For Ecological Complexity

There is a new view of nature emerging that replaces centuries of scientific reductionism. Instead of viewing nature simplistically as the sum of its parts, dominated by linear responses, and near equilibrium, this new view characterizes nature as complex, dominated by nonlinear relationships, with a variety of behaviors that are expressed at different hierarchical levels within an ecological organization that often operates close to disequilibrium (Waldrop 1992). Using the new model of nature, a reasonable management goal becomes one of maintaining the complexity inherent in natural ecosystems. This is not venerating the notion that "nature knows best," but this model does suggest there are many lessons that can be learned from unmanaged ecosystems and then applied to managing ecosystems for economic, social, and ecologic benefits.

Specific prescriptions for maintaining complexity will depend on the management objectives and the ecosystem. However, some general strategies have wide application. At the stand and landscape level, complexity involves composition and structure as well as function (process). Stands of mixed species composition can be used to achieve a variety of nontimber and timber objectives, such as enhanced soil fertility, fewer problems with insects and pathogens, and improved long-term forest productivity. Vertical structure includes the number, density, composition, and height of different vegetative layers. Creating multi-structured stands by developing species mixtures and retaining snags, other coarse woody debris, and multiple cohorts can enhance both the compositional and structural diversity of forests (O'Hara 1998, Palik and Zasada 2003). Specific examples include maintaining spruce and fir in the understory of aspen forests in the Great Lakes region or retaining green trees as canopy residuals in Douglas-fir forests in the Pacific Northwest to enhance avian diversity (Hansen and Hounihan 1996).

Despite a common perception that uneven-aged management is a "kinder and gentler" forestry, it is not necessarily a panacea for protecting ecological diversity. Uneven-aged management tends to favor shade-tolerant trees and, furthermore, repeated entries may result in damage to the residual stand, compact the soil, and disturb understory species (Kent et al., in press). Uneven-aged management also requires maintaining an extensive road system that fragments the forest, creating dispersal corridors for some species and barriers for others (Forman et al. 2003).

Silviculturists have focused primarily on commercial tree species—a small but important part of the forest ecosystem. There is a marked difference between our knowledge about producing timber and the knowledge needed to sustain other outputs and values gained from the forest. This is not to suggest that we know all that needs to be known about producing wood; as Jack Rajala, Alan Lucier, and David Reed reminded us at the Silviculture Summit, much remains to be learned (see this volume). Producing more commercial wood more efficiently and producing higher quality wood remain important goals for silviculture. For understandable reasons, silviculturists have concentrated on those parts of forest eco-systems that provide direct benefits to humans, while those things that make ecosystems work have received much less attention. Managing to maintain complexity or managing for aesthetics may seem

incompatible with maximizing wood production, but when viewed in the long term, conflicts become less apparent and even irrelevant. If managing for complexity maintains or enhances long-term forest productivity, then perceived conflicts between economic efficiency and ecologic sustainability become less onerous.

Conclusion

The reasons for applying silvicultural systems are expanding. In addition to growing wood, stake-holders now include aesthetics, sustainability, diversity, and conservation as measures of success (Cornett, Fernholz; this volume). A spatial perspective is helpful when applying silviculture techniques to achieve these broadening objectives. Without this perspective, the cumulative effects of multiple treatments in space and time can not be fully appreciated. While economic factors often promote the simplification of composition and structure in forest stands and landscapes, an "ecological approach" stresses managing for variety and complexity.

It will be necessary to develop many silvicultural systems to accommodate the many demands being placed on forest ecosystems, the great variety in ecosystem conditions, and the wide range of management goals that exist. As a result, a clear distinction between even- and uneven-aged systems will become less apparent. The limitations that we create through the rigid application of existing silvicultural systems limit our ability to adjust to changing needs and meet a broader set of goals through silviculture. Resource management is all about making better choices in a finite world; silviculture will be viewed as relevant when it helps us make better choices.

Literature Cited

Aplet, G.H.; Laven, R.D.; Smith, F.W. 1988. *Patterns of community dynamics in Colorado Engelmann spruce-subalpine fir forests.* Ecology. 69: 312-319.

Bratton, S.P. 1994. *Logging and fragmentation of broadleaved deciduous forests. Are we asking the right ecological questions?* Conservation Biology. 8: 295-297.

Cornett, M. 2004.
Silvicultural research needs in the Lake States: The Nature Conservancy Perspective. In: Palik, Brian; Levy, Louise, eds. Proceedings of the Great Lakes silviculture summit. Gen. Tech. Rep. NC-254. U.S. Department of Agriculture, Forest Service, North Central Research Station: 24-27.

Fernholz, K. 2004.
Small-scale, private lands forestry in the Lake States. In: Palik, Brian; Levy, Louise, eds. Proceedings of the Great Lakes silviculture summit. Gen. Tech. Rep. NC-254. U.S. Department of Agriculture, Forest Service, North Central Research Station: 28-32.

Forman, R.T.T.; *et al.* 2003.
Road ecology, science and solutions. Washington, DC: Island Press. 481 p.

Franklin, J.F.; Forman, R.T.T. 1987.
Creating landscape patterns by forest cutting: ecological consequences and principles. Landscape Ecology. 1: 5-18.

Hansen, A.J.; Hounihan, P. 1996.
Canopy tree retention and avian diversity in the Oregon Cascades. In: Szaro, R.C.; Johnston, D.W., eds. Biodiversity in managed landscapes, theory and practice. Oxford, UK: Oxford University Press: 401-421.

Kent, L.S.; Crow, T.R.; Buckley, D.S.; Nauertz, E.A.; Zasada, J.C. [In press].
Effects of harvesting and deer browsing on attributes of understory plants in a northern hardwood forest, upper Michigan, USA. Forest Ecology and Management.

Lucier, A.A. 2004.
Silviculture research priorities for strategic paper fibers in the Lake States. In: Palik, Brian; Levy, Louise, eds. Proceedings of the Great Lakes silviculture summit. Gen. Tech. Rep. NC-254. U.S. Department of Agriculture, Forest Service, North Central Research Station: 20-23.

Mladenoff, D.J.; White, M.A.; Pastor, J.; Crow, T.R. 1993.
Comparing spatial pattern in unaltered old-growth and disturbed forest landscapes. Ecological Applications. 3: 294-306.

O'Hara, K.L. 1998.
Silviculture for structural diversity, a new look at multiaged systems. Journal of Forestry. 96: 4-10.

Oliver, C.D.; Larson, B.C. 1996.
Forest stand dynamics. New York, NY: Wiley and Sons. 529 p.

Palik, B.; Zasada, J. 2003.
An ecological context for regenerating multi-cohort, mixed species red pine forests. Res. Note NC-382. St. Paul, MN: U.S. Department of Agriculture, Forest Service, North Central Research Station. 8 p.

Palik, B.; Levy, L.; Crow, T.R. 2004.
The Great Lakes Silviculture Summit: an introduction and organizing framework. In: Palik, Brian; Levy, Louise, eds. Proceedings of the Great Lakes silviculture summit. Gen. Tech. Rep. NC-254. U.S. Department of Agriculture, Forest Service, North Central Research Station: 1-4.

Rajala, J. 2004.
Silviculture for quality forests: a lumber and veneer perspective. In: Palik, Brian; Levy, Louise, eds. Proceedings of the Great Lakes silviculture summit. Gen. Tech. Rep. NC-254. U.S. Department of Agriculture, Forest Service, North Central Research Station: 33-37.

Reed, D.D. 2004.
The context for Great Lakes silviculture in the 21st century. In: Palik, Brian; Levy, Louise, eds. Proceedings of the Great Lakes silviculture summit. Gen. Tech. Rep. NC-254. U.S. Department of Agriculture, Forest Service, North Central Research Station: 15-19.

Riitters, K.; Wickham, J.; O'Neill, R.; *et al.* 2000.
Global-scale patterns of forest fragmentation. Conservation Ecology. 4: [online] http://www.consecol.org.vol4/iss2/art3.

Seymour, R.S. 2004.
Silviculture: lessons from our past, thoughts about the future. In: Palik, Brian; Levy, Louise, eds. Proceedings of the Great Lakes silviculture summit. Gen. Tech. Rep. NC-254. U.S. Department of Agriculture, Forest Service, North Central Research Station: 5-14.

Smith, D.M. 1962.
The practice of silviculture. New York, NY: Wiley and Sons. 578 p.

Tyrrell, L.E.; Crow, T.R. 1994.
Structural characteristics of old-growth hemlock-hardwood forests in relation to age. Ecology. 75: 294-306.

Wade, T.G.; Riitters, K.H.; Wickham, J.D.; Jones, K.B. 2003.
Distribution and causes of global forest fragmentation. Conservation Ecology. 7: [online] http://www.consecol.org.vol7/iss2/art7.

Waldrop, M. 1992.
Complexity: the emerging science at the edge of order and chaos. New York, NY: Simon and Schuster. 380 p.

A Research Agenda For Silviculture In The Great Lakes Region

Introduction

The Great Lakes Silviculture Summit took place in April 2003 at Michigan Technological University. The primary audience of the summit included institutional representatives who define needs and set policy regarding silvicultural approaches and practice, as well as researchers working in silviculture or related disciplines.

An overarching goal of the summit was to develop and strengthen a collaborative research network that focuses on priority silvicultural information needs of various "user groups," i.e., those that implement silviculture on the ground. A first step in developing this network was to obtain a clear message from decisionmakers about their needs.

A desired outcome for the summit was the development of a research agenda from topics identified and supported by summit participants. Our intention is that this agenda be used to articulate and prioritize informational needs for silviculture and related disciplines to funding agencies and to organizations that allocate internal resources to silviculture research.

We present the research agenda by organizing information needs within the context of our landscape spectrum model of forest management (see below and Palik et al., this volume). Using this approach, we identified where along the nodes of the management spectrum (intensive management, integrated management, reserve management) the informational needs lie.

For this synthesis, we relied on information needs expressed during presentations by the various "user group" representatives, along with their contributed papers, if they provided one (see this volume). The presenters were selected to represent six different perspectives on institutional management goals or objectives, including: 1) *pulp and paper production*, 2) *saw log and veneer log production*, 3) *nonindustrial private forest management*, 4) *conservation management*, 5) *Federal forest management*, and 6) *State forest management*. Before the summit, invited presenters were asked to determine and summarize the needs for the "type of organization" they represent, rather the needs of their specific organization. In this way, we hoped that the research agenda would be broadly inclusive of information needs in the region.

The research agenda also is developed from comments by summit participants, as recorded during breakout sessions. Moreover, we drew upon views expressed by a panel of invited responders representing major research and management organizations in the region (see appendix).

We attempted to identify dominant themes, i.e., information needs that clearly stood out as being important to the overall summit group. Dominant themes were repeated, although not necessarily verbatim, by multiple participants in a breakout session, in multiple breakout sessions, and by one or more invited speakers or panel members. Note that some stated needs may be included under multiple management nodes (e.g., production and integrated management). This occurred when the research need, as expressed by participants, clearly pertained to more than one node.

Research Needs Across the Landscape Spectrum

Our summary of silvicultural information needs can be articulated as a comprehensive research agenda by organizing around nodes of the "landscape spectrum" model in figure 1. Definitions of the nodes in our model are specific to our use. Others may define these nodes differently.

About The Authors:

Brian Palik, Project Leader, USDA Forest Service, North Central Research Station, Grand Rapids, MN; e-mail: bpalik@fs.fed.us

Louise Levy, Project Leader, Sustainable Forests Education Cooperative, University of Minnesota, Cloquet, MN; e-mail: llevy@umn.edu

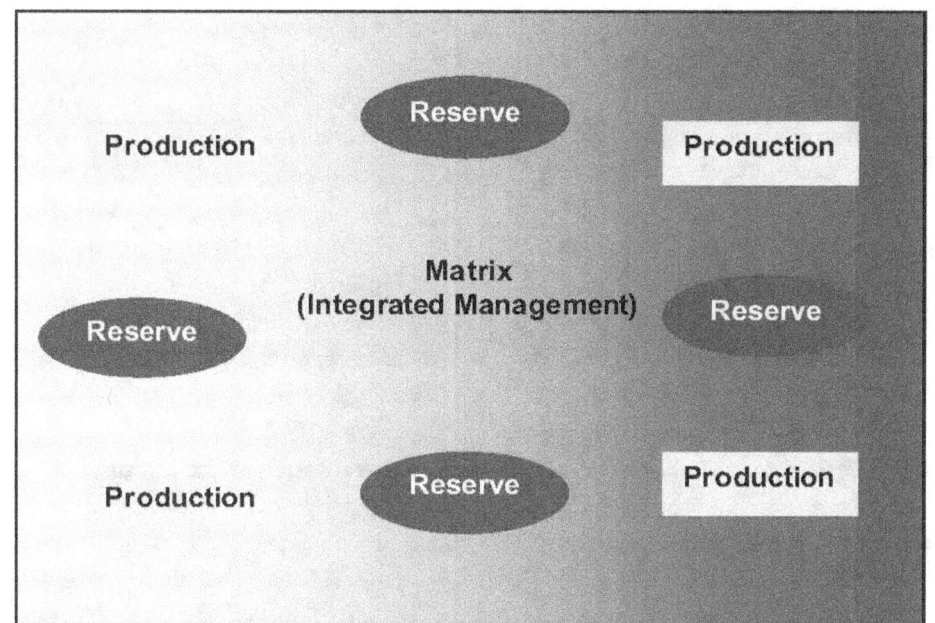

Figure 1. —A spectrum model of forest use allocation (adapted from Seymour and Hunter 1999). Production and reserve forests are embedded within a matrix managed for integration of ecological and production goals.

By our definition, the sole goal of production management is to maximize wood or fiber growth and yield without compromising the long-term sustainability of the production system. Managing for biological diversity or ecological complexity is not a stated objective for production systems, although there could be realized, but unplanned, ecological amenities associated with this management.

The sole goal for reserve management is to sustain (or restore) native biological diversity and ecological complexity in amounts and patterns deemed appropriate, given a selected benchmark for comparison. Commodity timber management is not an objective for reserves, although it could be a byproduct of this management, for instance, by thinning overstocked stands during restoration.

Goals and desired conditions for the matrix are diverse, as are the silvicultural approaches used to achieve them. Consequently, research needs for the matrix are equally diverse. They will integrate and balance production and ecological objectives to varying degrees depending on many factors, including landowner or stakeholder goals, landscape position, and current conditions.

The Research Agenda

A research agenda for production silviculture

The research agenda for production silviculture is driven largely by information needs for production of bulk fiber; however, needs related to sawtimber production, largely of softwoods for dimensional lumber, also figured prominently (see related paper in this volume). One dominant theme emerged: the need for information on *management systems that better realize the productive potential of species and sites.* This theme surfaced at least 12 times during breakout discussion, an order of magnitude more then any other topic. Specific information needs relative to this theme include systems to maximize and sustain production, realizing the potential to maximize production at various scales, under-standing the limiting factors to production, realizing production potential of mixed-species systems, predicting the cumulative effects of repeated management actions, and determining what actions are affordable and practical.

Additional information needs for production management include:

1. *Aspen and hybrid poplar management for fiber.*

    —Harvest prescriptions that increase the aspen component on desired sites

—Genetic selection, breeding, biotechnology, and plantation establishment

—Improved aspen growth and yield models including interactions of site, stocking, and fertilization

—Systems for improving wood quality

—Development of integrated management systems for hybrid poplar inclusive of weed control, stand establishment, tree nutrition, and pest management

2. *Softwoods*:

—Strategic assessment of softwood supply options, e.g., increased production vs. increased imports

—Cost/benefit analysis of silvicultural options for maturing and overstocked softwood stands

—Softwood silviculture options including thinning and fertilization of pine, deployment of hybrid larch plantation systems, and options for increasing spruce and fir production in planted or natural stands

—Ecological implications, at multiple scales, of plantation management systems

3. *Hardwoods*:

—Growth and yield research that enables value growth projection as a function of site quality, stand density, and species composition

—Prescriptions that promote regeneration of high quality mixed-hardwood and softwood stands

—Reliable and cost-effective herbicide treatments to control sedge, grass, and invasive plant and animal species

—Reliable predictions of time windows for successful regeneration, based on effective deer population control measures and knowledge of natural population cycles

4. *Carbon sequestration*:

—Realizing the potential of sequestration in forest ecosystems

5. *Management systems*:

—Integrated, cost-effective management systems (e.g., nutrition, density management) that can better realize productive potential of Great Lakes species

—More or maintained demonstrations (e.g., experimental forests) of research on systems for production management

—Understanding the impacts of production systems on tree population genetics

A research agenda for integrative silviculture in the landscape matrix

As with production management, one dominant research theme for integrative (matrix) management emerged from summit speakers and participants: *the need for information on trade-offs or balances between ecological objectives and production objectives.* This theme surfaced at least 12 times during breakout discussions, an order of magnitude more then any other topic. Specific information needs related to this theme include under-standing the tradeoffs for wood productivity when managing for ecological complexity; being able to quantify ecological and productivity outputs on a common scale to better measure tradeoffs; research on the effects of complex structure (e.g., multicohort) and extended rotations on regeneration and growth and yield; cost analysis of damages from selective logging in multi-cohort stands and how to minimize damage; systems for quality hardwood management to increase economic potential of the matrix; systems to emulate natural disturbance.

Additional silvicultural informational needs for the matrix include:

1. *Forest composition and structure*:

—Methods for maintaining aspen as a component in mixed-species and multi-cohort stands

—Management systems for red pine/white pine or white pine/hemlock that incorporate multi-cohort structure and reintroduction of fire

2. *Growth and yield*:

—Growth and yield data for long-rotation management, especially red pine

—Hardwood growth and yield equations that respond to stand density
—Tools for projecting value growth of mixed-species stands

3. *Regeneration*:
   —Minimization of regeneration failures due to deer browsing and improvement of regeneration in winter deeryards
   —Methods for white pine restoration, including regeneration in the understory of established stands
   —Improved approaches for regeneration of "difficult species," like paper birch, white cedar, eastern hemlock

4. *Management systems*:
   —Options for maturing and overstocked softwood stands
   —Approaches for the NIPF; prescriptions that are efficient, effective, ecologically sustainable, and affordable on small ownerships
   —Approaches for improving ecological condition, wildlife habitat, and regeneration on small NIPF ownerships
   —Systems for maintaining biodiversity while ensuring a sustainable rate of economic return

5. *Invasive species*:
   —Understanding of how overstory treatment predisposes stands to invasion by exotic species (floral and faunal)
   —Herbicide treatments for eradication of invasive plant species

6. *Natural disturbance-based silviculture*:
   —Prescriptions that emulate natural disturbance processes and pathways
   —Factoring range of natural variation into site-level prescriptions

A research agenda for silviculture in ecological reserves

In part, the research agenda for reserve management is based on information needs *inferred* from several of the invited speakers. None of the invited speakers actually stated needs specific to reserve management. However, many informational needs, particularly for matrix management, are applicable to reserves. In contrast to the invited speakers, the summit participants were quite vocal about information needs relative to reserve management. Two somewhat related themes emerged. There is a strong regional interest in determining *if natural disturbance is sufficient to sustain reserves in a desired condition*. Stated another way, there is concern that no action is insufficient for sustaining reserve ecosystems. Related to this is an interest in *emulating natural disturbance with silviculture* in reserves. These themes surfaced at least eight times during breakout discussions. The second theme, which surfaced at least five times during breakout discussions, was the need to understand *systems for developing old-growth forest and perpetuating it over time on the landscape*.

Additional information needs for ecological reserves include:
1. *Regeneration*:
   —Approaches to minimize regeneration failures due to deer browsing and improving regeneration in winter deeryards
   —Improved approaches for regeneration of "difficult species," like paper birch, white cedar, eastern hemlock

2. *Invasive species*:
   —Herbicide treatments for eradication of invasive plant species
   —Understanding of how overstory condition and treatment predisposes stands to invasion by exotics/invasive species (floral and faunal)

3. *Conifer research needs*:
   —Methods for successful white pine restoration
   —Management systems for red pine/white pine or white pine/hemlock that incorporate multi-cohort structure and reintroduction of fire

4. *Management Systems*:
   —Approaches specific to the NIPL for improving ecological condition, wildlife habitat, and regeneration

—Silviculture prescriptions that emulate natural disturbance processes

Landscape integration of stand-scale silviculture

Several of the stated information needs, while related to silviculture, are better articulated as needs related to landscape-scale integration of stand-scale management. Most of the "user group" presenters articulated such a need, and it was clearly and repeatedly expressed by summit participants and the invited panel. One dominant theme emerged related to landscape integration: *how and where to allocate stand-level management for production systems and ecological reserves within the landscape matrix.* Related to this is the need to shift the perspective of individual landowners toward a landscape focus.

Additional information needs for landscape integration include:
- —Understanding of the potential of carbon sequestration in forested landscapes
- —Ecological implications, at multiple scales, of plantation management systems
- —Management approaches for landscapes of mixed ownership
- —Understanding of landscape context/ cumulative impacts of stand management
- —Sustainability of multiple objectives (biodiversity, timber production, aesthetics) at multiple scales
- —Methods to compare aesthetics with timber production, i.e., tradeoffs or multiple responses

General themes

Two additional themes surfaced repeatedly during small group and panel discussions; they are general themes and not clearly specific to nodes of the management spectrum (fig. 1). The themes include 1) an interest in *silviculture research cooperatives* as a method for increasing communication between researchers and managers; and 2)

maintaining and invigorating experimental and demonstration forests. Poor information and technology transfer is seen as a great hindrance to practicing new and better silviculture. Cooperatives are seen as an effective way of improving this communication. Experimental and demonstration forests are seen as places to support the testing of new ideas, but also to aid in information transfer. Summit participants viewed the Federal Government as the obvious regional entity that is best suited to maintain experimental forests and associated research over the long term.

Literature Cited

Seymour, R.S.; Hunter, M.L., Jr. 1999. *Principles of ecological forestry.* In: Hunter, M.L., Jr., ed. Managing biodiversity in forest ecosystems. Cambridge, UK: Cambridge University Press: 22-61.

APPENDIX

Great Lakes Silviculture Summit Panel Discussion

This document summarizes a panel discussion that took place at the Great Lakes Silviculture Summit. Before the summit, panel participants were given the questions listed below. Each was asked to consider the questions and the Summit presentations when formulating their panel comments. Panel speakers are identified with their respective comments.

Panel Questions:

❖ How do our regional research capacities and capabilities in silviculture match the issues, problems, and needs that were identified?

❖ What is your vision of a research agenda for silviculture during the next 5-10 years?

❖ What do we need to do that is different?

❖ What are the responsibilities of the various research and management agencies and institutions?

Panel Responses

Glenn Mroz, *Dean, School of Forestry and Wood Products, Michigan Technological University:*

● There are three types of people: those who do, those who watch, those who wondered what happened. Silviculture researchers and users need to be those who do.

● Main points:
  ♦ There are TRENDS shaping silviculture whether or not we like it: e.g., economics (the need to demonstrate productive capacity of land so that it's not managed by real estate interests; also need to keep landscape in larger chunks). Important questions include: What is the productive capacity of the land? What's affordable and practical?
  ♦ We need SOCIAL SCIENCE research in our silviculture research (e.g., how do we market who we are, what we do, what technology we use?).
  ♦ RESEARCH FUNDING – we need more and we need it now. How do we get it? How do we successfully secure what's still out there?
  ♦ TRAINING – can we train in 4 years the foresters we need? (e.g., look to medical schools for a different model of professional education and training, research programs, etc.)

Glenn Mroz, *Dean, School of Forestry and Wood Products, Michigan Technological University*

Linda Donoghue, *Director,*
USDA Forest Service,
North Central Research Station

Linda Donoghue, *Director, USDA Forest Service, North Central Research Station:*

- My lens: I am a funder of research **and** I have to sell research ideas to funders. Research proposals must reflect certain criteria.
- The seven criteria I use as a funder and which are used by the funders I approach:
  1. The USDA Forest Service must reflect the PRESIDENT'S PRIORITIES AND AGENDA (e.g., The Healthy Forest Initiative, Wildland Fire Protection, Homeland Security, Domestic Energy Production), reducing risk from invasive species (e.g., emerald ash borer), fire, forest fragmentation (social, economic and ecological issues), off-road vehicle use and corresponding impact.
  2. The USDA Forest Service is funded by CONGRESSIONAL APPROPRIATIONS. Funding requests need to reflect a larger collaborative effort and support the priorities of key members of the legislature and their constituents. (e.g., FIA, invasives, wildland fires, wilderness and recreation, timber harvest, forest planning.)
  3. Existing or new research must reflect COLLABORATION AND MULTIPLE PERSPECTIVES affecting the issue.
  4. Science must serve needs of MULTIPLE CUSTOMERS.
  5. Research must leverage INTELLECTUAL AND FINANCIAL CAPITAL of the USDA Forest Service.
  6. Research must address MULTIPLE SCALES in space and time.
  7. Science must focus on the most important social and scientific issues that have HIGH VALUE to decisionmakers and policymakers. High value science:
     - Produces tools that assist.
     - Can be used to formulate policy or adaptation strategies—helps people see the future.
     - Helps people evaluate policy options once they're on the table.
     - Helps people know how best to implement policy.
     - Helps people in crisis.
- Ask yourselves: What is the social and economic value of your work?

John Johnson,
MeadWestvaco Corporation

John Johnson, *MeadWestvaco Corporation:*

- In our quest for funding, we are forgetting how our research questions in the Great Lakes Region fit into national context. What is the FUNDING SOURCE and what concerns have been articulated by that source?
- ECONOMIC CRISIS—There is a need to produce more wood to support communities. Take this message to policymakers.
- HIGH END PRODUCTIVITY—Industry needs to show a reasonable rate of return for our land. Fiber production, high quality timber (saw logs). There doesn't seem to be enough interest in and attention to producing more fiber more economically in both the research and "general" community. What's a reasonable rate of return? What's a reasonable amount of risk?
- IMPACTS—we need more information on impacts of management decisions.
- AVOID RESTRICTING APPROPRIATE RESEARCH/MANAGEMENT.

Jenna Fletcher, *Policy Analyst, Minnesota Forest Resources Council:*

- The Minnesota Forest Resources Council has three main responsibilities: 1) oversee voluntary site level guidelines effort; 2) develop a landscape management program; 3) advise Governor and legislature on how best to manage Minnesota's forests. In this context, the FRC is a quasi user of silviculture research.
- LANDSCAPE-LEVEL PLANNING. The FRC has completed two landscape-level plans and is completing the remainder for the State of Minnesota. Key challenge: how to manage across ownership boundaries.
- RANGE OF NATURAL VARIATION: a good tool that needs to become more robust.
- How can silviculture help us incorporate MULTIPLE VALUES/INTERESTS into management plan(s)? How can silviculture help us be more multidisciplinary? ... Social scientists should have been included in this meeting.
- Silviculture's LINK TO POLICYMAKERS—we need it.
- Focus silviculture research on critical issues (i.e., issues critical to constituents).
- Global climate change is one of these pressing issues.

Jenna Fletcher, *Policy Analyst, Minnesota Forest Resources Council*

Darrell Zastrow, *Wisconsin Department of Natural Resources, Office of Forest Sciences:*

- How well does silviculture research capacity and capability match the issues and needs we have identified?
  - List of research needs is long—role of States generally focused on applied research and the technical transfer of results.
  - Prioritizing silvicultural applications relative to the long list of research needs is difficult and there is a NEED FOR COORDINATION between research groups.
  - In Wisconsin, we identified the top research needs within forestry in the mid-1990s, many of which were silviculture. We are again assessing these research needs based on a statewide forest planning process and this will be complete approximately 2005.
  - Silviculture researchers may not be connected well enough to the forestry community.
- What is your vision?
  - Vision includes the public determining and encouraging a research agenda—publics must understand the process by which we collaborate, invest, share results, and dynamically change in time.
- What do we need to do differently?
  - Determine and articulate CRITICAL SERVICES we provide to the public.
  - TECHNICAL TRANSFER-QUANTIFY VALUE ADDED—take time to talk—value the systems in universities vs. agencies and use funding sources. Continue connecting with the publics we serve.
- What are the responsibilities of various management agencies and institutions? How do they differ? How do they mesh?
  - NATIONAL CAPACITY for forest research—what is the coordination responsibility at the Federal level?
  - Partnerships and roles need more definition.
  - FOREST SERVICE is uniquely positioned to provide leadership—more dollars and people and larger scale responsibility—e.g., FIA, Research, S&PF, national forests.
  - DEMONSTRATION FORESTS, such as the Argonne in Wisconsin, are the most valued applied research example provided by the Forest Service. FS has a unique ability to do long-term applied research.
  - STATE RESPONSIBILITY is collaboration with universities and Federal agencies. Advocate for funding from State perspective and help implement research efforts.

Darrell Zastrow, *Wisconsin Department of Natural Resources, Office of Forest Sciences*

www.ingramcontent.com/pod-product-compliance
Lightning Source LLC
Chambersburg PA
CBHW080611290526
45790CB00007B/2731